Crochet
RAGDOLL FRIENDS

36 New Dolls to Make

SASCHA BLASE-VAN WAGTENDONK

STACKPOLE BOOKS

Essex, Connecticut
Blue Ridge Summit, Pennsylvania

STACKPOLE BOOKS

An imprint of Globe Pequot, the trade division of The Rowman & Littlefield Publishing Group, Inc.
4501 Forbes Blvd., Ste. 200
Lanham, MD 20706
www.rowman.com

Distributed by NATIONAL BOOK NETWORK
800-462-6420

This edition is an English translation of Gehaakte lappenpoppen 3 and Lappenpoppen haken a la Sascha © Kosmos Uitgevers & Sascha Blase-van Wagtendonk, Utrecht/Antwerpen.
Translation: Sascha Blase-van Wagtendonk.

Gehaakte lappenpoppen 3:
    Patterns: Sascha Blase-van Wagtendonk
    Graphic design: Villa Grafica
    Photography: Sterstijl, Esther Befort
    © 2018: Kosmos Uitgevers & Sascha Blase-van Wagtendonk, Utrecht/Antwerpen.

Lappenpoppen haken à la Sascha:
    Patterns: Sascha Blase-van Wagtendonk
    Graphic design: Sigrid Bliekendaal
    Illustrations: Sigrid Bliekendaal & Marjet Verhoef
    Photography: Sterstijl, Esther Befort
    © 2020: Kosmos Uitgevers & Sascha Blase-van Wagtendonk, Utrecht/Antwerpen.

We have made every effort to ensure the accuracy and completeness of these instructions. We cannot, however, be responsible for human error, typographical mistakes, or variations in individual work.

British Library Cataloguing in Publication Information available

Library of Congress Cataloging-in-Publication Data Available

ISBN 978-0-8117-7170-2 (paper : alk. paper)
ISBN 978-0-8117-7171-9 (electronic)

♾™ The paper used in this publication meets the minimum requirements of American National Standard for Information Sciences—Permanence of Paper for Printed Library Materials, ANSI/NISO Z39.48-1992.

First Edition

CONTENTS

PATTERNS

27

45

54

74

89

111

124

135

144

158

INTRODUCTION

An introduction is always a special piece of text. Even though it's the very first piece of text you read, it's always the last thing I write and a moment to reflect on a new book that is completely finished. It's so very special to finalize my third book that is translated to English and the first book that I have translated myself.

When I designed my first ragdoll (the crocodile) in 2014, I never dreamed that you would find my sixtieth ragdoll in this book and that the books would be available in four different languages!

In this sequel to *Crochet Ragdolls*, I added quite a lot of novelties to the designs, so you will find some new and special characteristics in the patterns in this book! There are patterns for a nice round pig, a leopard with real spots, an extra woolly llama, a sleeping bear with pajamas on, a cute hedgehog with real spines, and much more!

Have fun crocheting many more ragdolls!

Lots of love,
Sascha

Yarn Choices

· ·

The ragdolls in this book are all crocheted with Scheepjes Stone Washed, but you can basically use any yarn with a matching hook. There are a few things to keep in mind:

- Are you making a stuffed animal for a baby or a young child? Keep in mind that the cuddly toy can go into a baby's or young child's mouth and preferably choose a natural (cotton) yarn and embroidered rather than beaded eyes.

- Always use a thinner hook than you would normally choose for the yarn, so that there are no holes for the filling to come through.

To give you an idea of the effect that different types of yarn will have, this adorable litter of puppies is showing all different kinds of yarn!

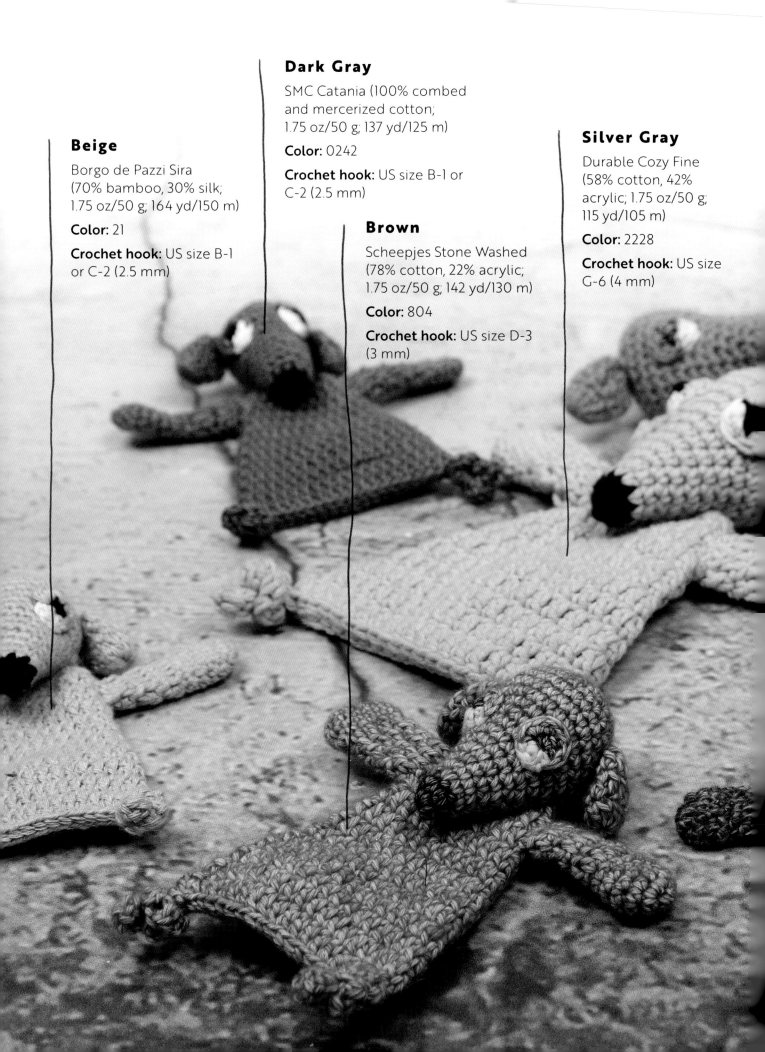

Beige

Borgo de Pazzi Sira
(70% bamboo, 30% silk;
1.75 oz/50 g; 164 yd/150 m)

Color: 21

Crochet hook: US size B-1
or C-2 (2.5 mm)

Dark Gray

SMC Catania (100% combed
and mercerized cotton;
1.75 oz/50 g; 137 yd/125 m)

Color: 0242

Crochet hook: US size B-1 or
C-2 (2.5 mm)

Brown

Scheepjes Stone Washed
(78% cotton, 22% acrylic;
1.75 oz/50 g; 142 yd/130 m)

Color: 804

Crochet hook: US size D-3
(3 mm)

Silver Gray

Durable Cozy Fine
(58% cotton, 42%
acrylic; 1.75 oz/50 g;
115 yd/105 m)

Color: 2228

Crochet hook: US size
G-6 (4 mm)

Yellow

Borgo de Pazzi Amore 160
(70% merino, 25% polyamide,
2% viscose, 2% acrylic, 1% poly-
ester; 1.75 oz/50 g; 175 yd/160 m)

Color: 113

Crochet hook: US size E-4
(3.5 mm)

Mottled Brown

Durable Forest (45% acrylic,
18% silk, 37% merino wool;
1.75 oz/50 g; 204.5 yd/187 m)

Color: 4015

Crochet hook: US size B-1
(2.25 mm)

Mottled Dark Gray

Borgo de Pazzi Clara
(65% wool, 35% cotton;
1.75 oz/50 g; 93 yd/85 m)

Color: 251

Crochet hook: US size H-8
(5 mm)

Mottled Beige

SMC Catania (100% cotton;
1.75 oz/50 g; 131 yd/120 m)

Color: 404

Crochet hook: US size B-1
or C-2 (2.5 mm)

Crochet Stitches

Magic Loop

Make a circle of the yarn by folding the loose end of the yarn behind the yarn attached to the skein. Now insert your crochet hook into the ring. Wrap the working yarn over your hook and pull the yarn through the ring. Hook 1 chain to secure the ring. Then hook the number of stitches in the ring as indicated in the pattern. Make sure that you hook around the strands of both the ring and the loose end of the yarn. When you have the desired number of stitches, pull the loose end tightly to close the ring. Then continue in pattern.

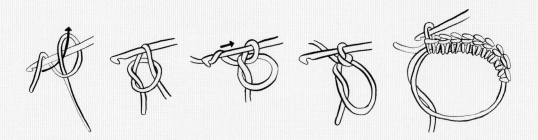

Abbreviations

Chain	ch
Slip stitch	sl st
Single crochet	sc
Half double crochet	hdc
Double crochet	dc
Triple crochet	tr
Single crochet 2 together	sc2tog
Double crochet 2 together	dc2tog
Front post double crochet	fpdc
Back post double crochet	bpdc

CHAIN (ch)

Wrap the working yarn from back to front over the crochet hook. Now pull the yarn through the loop on your hook, and you have made a chain stitch. Repeat for the desired number of chains.

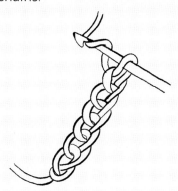

SLIP STITCH (sl st)

Insert the crochet hook from the front to the back and then under the yarn so that the working yarn is over your crochet hook. Now pull the yarn through the 2 loops on your hook, and you have made a slip stitch.

SINGLE CROCHET (sc)

Insert the crochet hook from the front to the back and wrap the working yarn over the hook from back to front. Now pull the yarn through the stitch. Wrap the yarn over the hook from back to front again and pull this through the 2 loops on your hook, and you have made a single crochet.

HALF DOUBLE CROCHET (hdc)

Wrap the working yarn from back to front over the crochet hook. Insert the crochet hook from the front to the back, wrap the working yarn over the hook from back to front, and then pull the yarn through the stitch. Make another wrap and pass it through the 3 loops on your hook, and you have made a half double crochet.

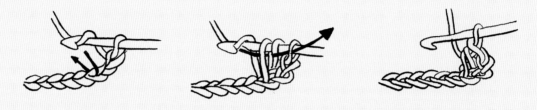

DOUBLE CROCHET (dc)

Wrap the working yarn from back to front over the crochet hook. Insert the crochet hook from the front to the back, wrap the yarn over the hook, and then pull the yarn through the stitch. Make another wrap and pass it through 2 of the loops on your hook. Then make another wrap and pull it through the last 2 loops on your hook, and you have made a double crochet.

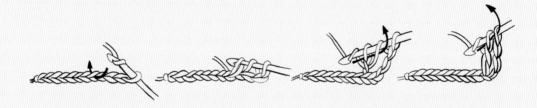

TRIPLE CROCHET (tr)

Wrap the yarn around the crochet hook 2 times from back to front. Insert the crochet hook from the front to the back, make a wrap and pull the yarn through the stitch, *make another wrap and pull it through 2 of the loops on your hook*, repeat from * to * 2 more times, and you have made a triple crochet.

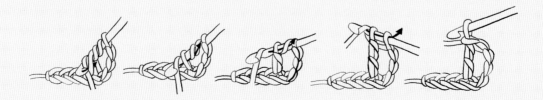

SINGLE CROCHET TOGETHER (sctog)

Insert the crochet hook from front to back in the next stitch. Wrap the working yarn from back to front over the crochet hook and pull the yarn through the stitch. Repeat these steps for the next stitch (or multiple stitches that you want to join). Finally, make a wrap and pull it through all the loops on your hook. You now have crocheted several stitches together, decreasing the total stitch count.

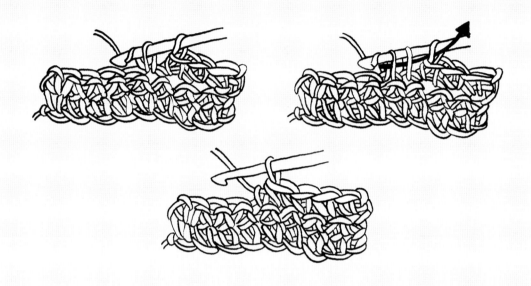

DOUBLE CROCHET TOGETHER (dctog)

Wrap the working yarn from back to front over the crochet hook. Insert the crochet hook from the front to the back in the next stitch. Make a wrap and pull it through the stitch, and then make another wrap and pull it through 2 of the loops on your hook. Repeat these steps for the next or possibly several stitches that you want to join. Finally, make a wrap and pull it through all the loops on your hook. You have now double crocheted several stitches together to make 1 stitch.

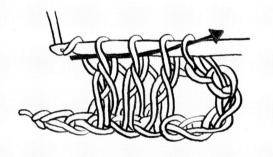
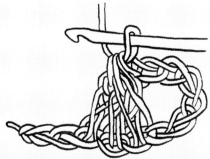

Tips and Tricks

- Many parts are worked in continuous rounds without closing, so it is useful to use a stitch marker.
- To change colors, work the last step of the stitch before the color change with the new color. For example, if the last stitch before a color change is a single crochet, work the last yarn over that you pull through two loops with the new color.
- In some patterns you change colors very often. Instead of fastening off after each round, you can carry the unused color along. You do this by holding the yarn of the color that you are not using along the top of the stitches you will crochet in and then crocheting around it.
- You can add all kinds of accessories to give the ragdolls an extra playful element. Think, for example, of a squeaker in a paw, a rattle in the head, a sheet of crinkly plastic in the body, or a teething ring in a hand.

Making the Body

||||\|| \||||\| ||||||||||\| || ||\|||\||||| \|\|||||\| \|||||||\| ||\

The bodies of the ragdolls are worked in the round, around a chain of stitches. Because this is not a common method, it can seem difficult, but it's actually quite simple. Below you will find the start of the body, explained in pictures and a drawing. This description is based on the number of starting chains for most large ragdolls. You'll start with fewer chain stitches for some of the large and all of the small ragdolls, but the method is the same.

1

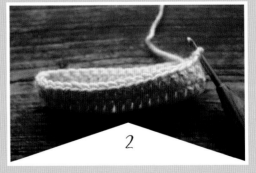
2

Round 1 (shown in orange)

- You always start with a chain; the exact number can be found in the instructions.
- Then you work 1 dc in the 3rd ch from your hook.
- You will work a dc in each chain until the last.
- In the last chain you'll work 3 dc.
- Then you continue on the other side of the chain.
- You'll work the instructed number of dc on the other side of the chain too.
- Finally, work 3 dc on the other corner and join the round with a sl st in the first dc.

Round 2 (shown in black)

- From the second round you'll always start with 2 chains; these do not count as the first dc, but are only meant to make height for the stitches that you are going to make.
- Because of the previous bullet point, you'll work the first dc in the same stitch as the ch 2.
- Then work the number of dc as described in the instructions.
- After this, increase by making 2 dc in 1 stitch.
- Then repeat the same number of dc as on the other side and increase in the last dc again, which you'll connect with a slip stitch in the first dc.

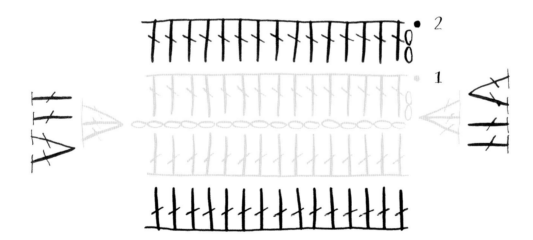

The following rounds all continue in the same way. You will see that all increases are stacked on top of each other; this is also a good way to check if you're doing it correctly. Depending on the hand in which you hold your hook and how tight you make your stitches, the body can sometimes have a tendency to twist. However, if you follow the method as described above and your stitch count is correct after each round, you can easily fold the body straight along the increase line at the end and sew it down this way.

Faces and Eyes

In this second book of ragdolls there is more variation in the faces. Although plastic safety eyes were used for all patterns in the previous book, this time you will also find instructions for different types of crochet eyes.

You can easily mix and match the eyes of all patterns and just have fun with it!

Don't be fooled by the term "safety eyes." When making a stuffed animal for a baby or young child, I really recommend using crochet or embroidered eyes, as the plastic kind can come off with all the dangers that come with that.

Putting It All Together

- - - - - - - - - - - - - - - - - -

Although not every ragdoll has exactly the same body parts, the way to put them together is identical.

1. For the large ragdolls, place both legs between the two layers at the bottom and close the body at the same time. For the little ones, don't attach legs, but sew the bottom in the same way, using the remaining yarn from the body.

2. Sew one arm to each side of the body as described in the instructions.

3. Sew the head to the body as described in the instructions.

LLAMA

DIFFICULTY LEVEL: 3 of 5

SIZE: 12.5 in (32 cm) tall

MATERIALS

Yarn: DK #3 light weight yarn; shown in Scheepjes Stone Washed
- Brown (Brown Agate 822): 142.5 yd (130 m)
- Light pink (Pink Quartzite 821): 76.5 yd (70 m)
- Scraps in blue, yellow, pink, and purple: 33 yd (30 m) each

Crochet hook: US size D-3 (3 mm)

Other:
- Brown with black safety eyes, 15 mm
- Fiberfill stuffing
- Needle and scissors

SPECIAL STITCH

Dctog-bobble (dc3tog-b or dc-5tog-b) = Work 3 (or 5) dc into 1 stitch (as if working a dctog, omitting the final yarn over and pull through of each stitch), finally pulling the last yarn over through all loops on hook to create a bobble.

HEAD

Rnd 1: With brown, start with a magic loop, 6sc in the loop. (6)

Rnd 2: 2sc in each stitch around. (12)

Rnd 3: *Dc3tog-b in next, 2sc in next*, repeat around. (18)

Note: The dc3tog-b tends to fall to the inside, so I like to pop them out after each round.

Rnd 4: *2sc in next, sc1, dc3tog-b in next*, repeat around. (24)

Rnd 5: *2sc in next, dc3tog-b in next, sc2*, repeat around. (30)

Rnd 6: *2sc in next, dc3tog-b in next, sc2, dc3tog-b in next*, repeat around. (36)

Rnd 7: *2sc in next, dc3tog-b in next, sc2, dc3tog-b in next, sc1*, repeat around. (42)

Rnd 8: *Sc1, dc3tog-b in next, sc2, dc3tog-b in next, sc2*, repeat around. (42)

Rnd 9: With light pink, sc1 in each stitch around. (42) Cut the brown yarn.

Rnd 10: Sc1 in each stitch around. (42)

Rnd 11: *Sc19, sc2tog*, repeat from * to * one more time. (40)

Rnds 12–13: Sc1 in each stitch around. (40)

Rnd 14: *Sc18, sc2tog*, repeat from * to * one more time. (38)

Rnds 15–16: Sc1 in each stitch around. (38)

Rnd 17: *Sc17, sc2tog*, repeat from * to * one more time. (36)

Rnd 18: Sc1 in each stitch around. (36)

Rnd 19: *Sc16, sc2tog*, repeat from * to * one more time. (34)

Rnd 20: Sc1 in each stitch around. (34)

Rnd 21: *Sc15, sc2tog*, repeat from * to * one more time. (32)

Rnd 22: Sc1 in each stitch around. (32)

Rnd 23: *Sc14, sc2tog*, repeat from * to * one more time. (30)

Rnd 24: Sc1 in each stitch around. (30)

Rnd 25: *Sc13, sc2tog*, repeat from * to * one more time. (28)

Rnd 26: *Sc12, sc2tog*, repeat from * to * one more time. (26)

Rnd 27: *Sc11, sc2tog*, repeat from * to * one more time. (24)

Attach safety eyes between rnds 15 and 16, 11 stitches apart.

Rnd 28: *Sc2, sc2tog*, repeat from * to * around. (18) Stuff the head.

Rnd 29: *Sc1, sc2tog*, repeat from * to * around. (12)

Cut a long tail, weave through the 12 remaining stitches, pull tight, and weave in end.

EARS (MAKE 2)

Rnd 1: With brown, start with a magic loop, ch2 (doesn't count as first dc now and throughout), 6dc in the loop, sl st in first dc. (6)

Rnd 2: Ch2, *1dc, 2dc in next*, repeat from * to * around, sl st in first dc. (9)

Rnd 3: Ch2, *dc2, 2dc in next*, repeat from * to * around, sl st in first dc. (12)

Rnd 4: Ch2, *dc3, 2dc in next*, repeat from * to * around, sl st in first dc. (15)

Rnd 5: Ch2, *dc4, 2dc in next*, repeat from * to * around, sl st in first dc. (18)

Cut a long tail, fold the bottom of the ear in half, sew in place, and attach to head on each side of the head in rnd 7. Take small pieces of yarn (approx. 8 in or 20 cm) in purple, pink, yellow, and blue. Fold in half and, with your hook, pull through the top of the ear. Now pull the loose pieces of yarn through the loop, pull tight, and cut the pieces of yarn so they are approximately 1.5 in (3.5 cm).

BODY

Rnd 1: With brown, ch16, dc1 in 3rd ch from hook, dc12, 3dc in last, continue in the other side of the chains, dc13, 3dc in last, sl st in first dc. (32)
Rnd 2: Ch2 (doesn't count as first dc now and throughout), *dc15, 2dc in next*, repeat from * to * one more time, sl st in first dc. (34)
Rnd 3: Ch2, dc2, dc5tog-b in next, dc3, dc5tog-b in next, dc3, dc5tog-b in next, dc5, 2dc in next, dc16, 2dc in next, sl st in first dc. (36)
Rnd 4: Ch2, *dc17, 2dc in next*, repeat from * to * one more time, sl st in first dc. (38)
Rnd 5: Ch2, dc1, dc5tog-b in next, *dc3, dc5tog-b in next*, repeat from * to * 2 more times, dc4, 2dc in next, dc18, 2dc in next, sl st in first dc. (40)
Rnd 6: Ch2, *dc19, 2dc in next*, repeat from * to * one more time, sl st in first dc. (42)
Rnd 7: Ch2, dc4, dc5tog-b in next, *dc3, dc5tog-b in next*, repeat from * to * 2 more times, dc3, 2dc in next, dc20, 2dc in next, sl st in first dc. (44)
Rnd 8: Ch2, *dc21, 2dc in next*, repeat from * to * one more time, sl st in first dc. (46)

Rnd 9: Ch2, dc2, dc5tog-b in next, *dc3, dc5tog-b in next*, repeat from * to * 3 more times, dc3, 2dc in next, dc22, 2dc in next, sl st in first dc. (48)
Rnd 10: Ch2, *dc23, 2dc in next*, repeat from * to * one more time, sl st in first dc. (50)
Rnd 11: Ch2, dc1, dc5tog-b in next, *dc3, dc5tog-b in next*, repeat from * to * 4 more times, dc2, 2dc in next, dc24, 2dc in next, sl st in first dc. (52)
Rnd 12: Ch2, *dc25, 2dc in next*, repeat from * to * one more time, sl st in first dc. (54)
Rnd 13: With purple, ch2, *dc26, 2dc in next*, repeat from * to * one more time, sl st in first dc. (56) You can cut the yarn and weave in end; you can cut the yarn after each rnd of the next new colors too.
Rnd 14: With pink, ch2, *dc27, 2dc in next*, repeat from * to * one more time, sl st in first dc. (58)
Rnd 15: With yellow, ch2, *dc28, 2dc in next*, repeat from * to * one more time, sl st in first dc. (60)
Rnd 16: With blue, ch2, *dc29, 2dc in next*, repeat from * to * one more time, sl st in first dc. (62)
Rnd 17: With brown, ch2, *dc30, 2dc in next*, repeat from * to * one more time, sl st in first dc. (64)
Rnd 18: Ch2, *dc31, 2dc in next*, repeat from * to * one more time, sl st in first dc. (66)
Rnd 19: Ch2, *dc32, 2dc in next*, repeat from * to * one more time, sl st in first dc. (68)

Cut a long tail to close the body later. Fold the body in line with the increases to make the belly straight.

ARMS (MAKE 2)

Rnd 1: With light pink, start with a magic loop, ch2, 6dc in the loop, sl st in first dc. (6)

Rnd 2: Ch2 (doesn't count as first dc now and throughout), *dc1, 2dc in next*, repeat from * to * around, sl st in first dc. (9)

Rnd 3: Ch2, dc1 in each stitch around, sl st in first dc. (9)

Rnd 4: With brown, ch2, 2dc in each stitch around, sl st in first dc. (18) You can cut the light pink yarn.

Rnd 5: Ch2, dc2tog, dc1 in each stitch around, sl st in first dc. (17)

Rnd 6: Ch2, dc1 in each stitch around, sl st in first dc. (17)

Rnd 7: Ch2, dc2tog, dc1 in each stitch around, sl st in first dc. (16)

Rnd 8: Ch2, dc1 in each stitch around, sl st in first dc. (16)

Rnd 9: Ch2, dc2tog, dc1 in each stitch around, sl st in first dc. (15)

Rnd 10: Ch2, dc1 in each stitch around, sl st in first dc. (15)

Rnd 11: Ch2, dc2tog, dc1 in each stitch around, sl st in first dc. (14)

Rnd 12: Ch2, dc1 in each stitch around, sl st in first dc. (14)

Rnd 13: Ch2, dc2tog, dc1 in each stitch around, sl st in first dc. (13)

Cut a long tail to attach arms later.

LEGS (MAKE 2)

Crochet rnds 1–9 as for arms, cut yarn and weave in ends.

PUTTING IT ALL TOGETHER

- Take the body and place both legs between the bottom two layers. With the remaining yarn from the body, sew across the seam with the legs in between. This way you close the bottom and assemble pieces at the same time.
- Sew an arm to each side of the body between rnds 1 and 3.
- With the brown yarn, embroider a nose in the center of the head between rnds 22 and 29, as illustrated.
- Finally, sew rnd 19 of the head to rnd 1 of the body.

BABY LLAMA

DIFFICULTY LEVEL: 3 of 5

SIZE: 6.5 in (17 cm) tall

MATERIALS

Yarn: DK #3 light weight yarn; shown in Scheepjes Stone Washed
- Brown (Brown Agate 822): 109.5 yd (100 m)
- Light pink (Pink Quartzite 821): 22 yd (20 m)

Crochet hook: US size D-3 (3 mm)

Other:
- Black and brown safety eyes, 12 mm
- Fiberfill stuffing
- Needle and scissors

SPECIAL STITCH

Dctog-bobble (dc3tog-b or dc5tog-b) = Work 3 (or 5) dc into 1 stitch (as if working a dctog omitting the final yarn over and pull through of each stitch), finally pulling the last yarn over through all loops on hook to create a bobble.

HEAD

Rnd 1: With brown, start with a magic loop, 6sc in the loop. (6)

Rnd 2: 2sc in each stitch around. (12)

Rnd 3: *Dc3tog-b, 2sc in next*, repeat around. (18)

Note: The dc3tog-b tends to fall to the inside, so I like to pop them out after each round.

Rnd 4: *2sc in next, sc1, dc3tog-b*, repeat around. (24)

Rnd 5: *2sc in next, dc3tog-b, sc2*, repeat around. (30)

Rnd 6: *Sc1, dc3tog-b, sc2, dc3tog in 1 stitch*, repeat around. (30)

Rnd 7: With light pink (you can cut the brown yarn), sc1 in each stitch around. (30)

Rnd 8: Sc1 in each stitch around. (30)

Rnd 9: *Sc13, sc2tog*, repeat from * to * one more time. (28)

Rnd 10: Sc1 in each stitch around. (28)

Rnd 11: *Sc12, sc2tog*, repeat from * to * one more time. (26)

Rnd 12: Sc1 in each stitch around. (26)

Rnd 13: *Sc11, sc2tog*, repeat from * to * one more time. (24)

Rnd 14: Sc1 in each stitch around. (24)

Rnd 15: *Sc10, sc2tog*, repeat from * to * one more time. (22)

Rnd 16: Sc1 in each stitch around. (22)

Rnd 17: *Sc9, sc2tog*, repeat from * to * one more time. (20)

Rnd 18: Sc1 in each stitch around. (20)

Rnd 19: *Sc8, sc2tog*, repeat from * to * one more time. (18) Attach safety eyes between rnds 11 and 12, 6 stitches apart, and stuff the head.

Rnd 20: *Sc1, sc2tog*, repeat from * to * around. (12)

Rnd 21: *Sc2tog*, repeat from * to * around. (6)

Cut a long tail, weave through the 6 remaining stitches, pull tight, and weave in end.

EARS (MAKE 2)

Rnd 1: With brown, start with a magic loop, ch2 (doesn't count as first dc now and throughout), 6dc in the loop, sl st in first dc. (6)

Rnd 2: Ch2, *2dc, 2dc in next*, repeat from * to * around, sl st in first dc. (8)

Rnd 3: Ch2, *3dc, 2dc in next*, repeat from * to * around, sl st in first dc. (10)

Cut a long tail, fold the bottom of the ear in half, sew in place, and attach to head on each side of the head in rnd 5.

BODY

Rnd 1: With brown, ch11, dc1 in 3rd ch from hook, dc7, 3dc in last, continue in the other side of the chains, dc8, 3dc in last, sl st in first dc. (22)

Rnd 2: Ch2 (doesn't count as first dc now and throughout), *dc10, 2dc in next*, repeat from * to * one more time, sl st in first dc. (24)

Rnd 3: Ch2, dc2, *dc5tog-b, dc2*, repeat from * to * 2 more times, 2dc in next, dc11, 2dc in next, sl st in first dc. (26)

Rnd 4: Ch2, *dc12, 2dc in next*, repeat from * to * one more time, sl st in first dc. (28)

Rnd 5: Ch2, dc1, *dc5tog-b, dc2*, repeat from * to * 3 more times, 2dc in next, dc13, 2dc in next, sl st in first dc. (30)

Rnd 6: Ch2, *dc14, 2dc in next*, repeat from * to * one more time, sl st in first dc. (32)

Rnd 7: Ch2, dc1, dc5tog-b, *dc2, dc5tog-b, repeat from * to * 3 more times, dc1, 2dc in next, dc15, 2dc in next, sl st in first dc. (34)

Rnd 8: Ch2, *dc16, 2dc in next*, repeat from * to * one more time, sl st in first dc. (36)

Rnd 9: Ch2, dc3, dc5tog-b, *dc2, dc5tog-b, repeat from * to * 2 more times, dc4, 2dc in next, dc17, 2dc in next, sl st in first dc. (38)

Rnd 10: Ch2, *dc18, 2dc in next*, repeat from * to * one more time, sl st in first dc. (40)

Rnd 11: Ch2, dc3, dc5tog-b, *dc2, dc5tog-b, repeat from * to * 3 more times, dc3, 2dc in next, dc19, 2dc in next, sl st in first dc. (42)

Rnd 12: Ch2, *dc20, ch14, dc1 in 3rd ch from hook, dc1 in each of the remaining 11 chains, 2dc in next dc of rnd 11*, repeat one more time, sl st in first dc.

Cut a long tail to close the body later.

ARMS (MAKE 2)

Rnd 1: With light pink, start with a magic loop, ch2 (doesn't count as first dc now and throughout), 6dc in the loop, sl st in first dc. (6)

Rnd 2: Ch2, *dc2, 2dc in next*, repeat from * to * around, sl st in first dc. (8)

Rnd 3: With brown (you can cut the light pink yarn), ch2, *dc1, 2dc in next*, repeat around, sl st in first dc. (12)

Rnd 4: Ch2, dc2tog, dc1 in each stitch around, sl st in first dc. (11)

Rnd 5: Ch2, dc1 in each stitch around, sl st in first dc. (11)

Rnd 6: Ch2, dc2tog, dc1 in each stitch around, sl st in first dc. (10)

Rnd 7: Ch2, dc1 in each stitch around, sl st in first dc. (10)

Cut a long tail to attach arms later.

PUTTING IT ALL TOGETHER

- Fold the body in line with the increases to make the belly straight and sew closed with the remaining yarn. Tie a knot in the corners to form the feet.
- Sew an arm to each side of the body between rnds 1 and 2.
- Sew the bottom of rnd 14 of the head to rnd 1 of the body.
- Finally, with the brown yarn, embroider a nose in the center of the head between rnds 17 and 20, as pictured.

DACHSHUND

DIFFICULTY LEVEL: 2 of 5

SIZE: 9.5 in (24 cm) tall

MATERIALS

Yarn: DK #3 light weight yarn; shown in Scheepjes Stone Washed
- Brown (Brown Agate 822): 164 yd (150 m)
- Black (Black Onyx 803): 54.5 yd (50 m)
- Small amount of white

Crochet hook: US size D-3 (3 mm)

Other:
- Fiberfill stuffing
- Needle and scissors

HEAD

Rnd 1: With black, start with a magic loop, 6sc in the loop. (6)

Rnd 2: 2sc in each stitch around. (12)

Rnds 3–4: Sc1 in each stitch around. (12)

Rnd 5: With brown, *sc2, 2sc in next stitch*, repeat around. (16) You can cut the black yarn.

Rnds 6–7: Sc1 in each stitch around. (16)

Rnd 8: *Sc3, 2sc in next stitch*, repeat around. (20)

Rnds 9–10: Sc1 in each stitch around. (20)

Rnd 11: *Sc4, 2sc in next stitch*, repeat around. (24)

Rnds 12–13: Sc1 in each stitch around. (24)

Rnd 14: *Sc5, 2sc in next stitch*, repeat around. (28)

Rnds 15–16: Sc1 in each stitch around. (28)

Rnd 17: *Sc3, 2sc in next stitch*, repeat around. (35)

Rnd 18: Sc1 in each stitch around. (35)

Rnd 19: *Sc4, 2sc in next stitch*, repeat around. (42)

Rnds 20–24: Sc1 in each stitch around. (42)

Rnd 25: *Sc5, sc2tog*, repeat around. (36)

Rnd 26: *Sc4, sc2tog*, repeat around. (30)

Rnd 27: *Sc3, sc2tog*, repeat around. (24)

Rnd 28: *Sc2, sc2tog*, repeat around. (18) Stuff the head carefully.

Rnd 29: *Sc1, sc2tog*, repeat around. (12)

Rnd 30: *Sc2tog*, repeat around. (6)

Cut a long tail, weave through the 6 remaining stitches, pull tight, and leave the end to sew the head to the body later.

EARS (MAKE 2)

Rnd 1: With black, start with a magic loop, ch2 (doesn't count as first dc now and throughout), 12dc in the loop, sl st in first dc. (12)
Rnd 2: With brown, ch2, *dc1, 2dc in next*, repeat around, sl st in first dc. (18) You can cut the black yarn.
Rnd 3: Ch2, dc1 in each stitch around, sl st in first dc. (18)
Rnd 4: Ch2, *dc4, dc2tog*, repeat around, sl st in first dc. (15)
Rnd 5: Ch2, *dc3, dc2tog*, repeat around, sl st in first dc. (12)
Rnd 6: Ch2, *dc2tog*, repeat around, sl st in first dc. (6)

Cut a long tail to sew on head later.

BODY

Rnd 1: With brown, ch14, dc1 in 3rd ch from hook, dc10, 3dc in last, continue in the other side of the chains, dc11, 3dc in last, sl st in first dc. (28)
Rnd 2: Ch2 (doesn't count as first dc now and throughout), *dc13, 2dc in next*, repeat from * to * one more time, sl st in first dc. (30)
Rnd 3: Ch2, dc1 in each stitch around, sl st in first dc. (30)
Rnd 4: Ch2, *dc14, 2dc in next*, repeat from * to * one more time, sl st in first dc. (32)
Rnd 5: Ch2, dc1 in each stitch around, sl st in first dc. (32)
Rnd 6: Ch2, *dc15, 2dc in next*, repeat from * to * one more time, sl st in first dc. (34)
Rnd 7: Ch2, dc1 in each stitch around, sl st in first dc. (34)

Rnd 8: Ch2, *dc16, 2dc in next*, repeat from * to * one more time, sl st in first dc. (36)
Rnd 9: Ch2, dc1 in each stitch around, sl st in first dc. (36)
Rnd 10: Ch2, *dc17, 2dc in next*, repeat from * to * one more time, sl st in first dc. (38)
Rnd 11: Ch2, dc1 in each stitch around, sl st in first dc. (38)
Rnd 12: Ch2, *dc18, 2dc in next*, repeat from * to * one more time, sl st in first dc. (40)
Rnd 13: Ch2, dc1 in each stitch around, sl st in first dc. (40)
Rnd 14: Ch2, *dc19, 2dc in next*, repeat from * to * one more time, sl st in first dc. (42)
Rnd 15: Ch2, dc1 in each stitch around, sl st in first dc. (42)
Rnd 16: Ch2, *dc20, 2dc in next*, repeat from * to * one more time, sl st in first dc. (44)
Rnd 17: Ch2, dc1 in each stitch around, sl st in first dc. (44)
Rnd 18: Ch2, *dc21, 2dc in next*, repeat from * to * one more time, sl st in first dc. (46)
Rnd 19: Ch2, dc1 in each stitch around, sl st in first dc. (46)

Cut a long tail to close the body later. Fold the body in line with the increases to make the belly straight.

ARMS (MAKE 2)

Rnd 1: With brown, start with a magic loop, 6sc in the loop. (6)
Rnd 2: 2sc in each stitch around. (12)
Rnd 3: *Sc1, 2sc in next stitch*, repeat around. (18)
Rnds 4–6: Sc1 in each stitch around. (18)
Rnd 7: *Sc4, sc2tog*, repeat around. (15)
Rnds 8–9: Sc1 in each stitch around. (15)
Rnd 10: Sl st 1, ch2 (doesn't count as first dc now and throughout), dc1 in each stitch around, sl st in first dc. (15)
Rnd 11: Ch2, dc2tog, dc1 in each stitch around, sl st in first dc. (14)
Rnd 12: Ch2, dc1 in each stitch around, sl st in first dc. (14)
Rnd 13: Ch2, dc2tog, dc1 in each stitch around, sl st in first dc. (13)

Cut a long tail to attach arms later.

LEGS (MAKE 2)

Rnd 1: With brown, start with a magic loop, ch2 (doesn't count as first dc now and throughout), 12dc in the loop, sl st in first dc. (12)
Rnds 2–5: Ch2, dc1 in each stitch around, sl st in first dc. (12)

Cut yarn and weave in ends.

TAIL

Rnd 1: With black, start with a magic loop, ch2 (doesn't count as first dc now and throughout), 8dc in the loop, sl st in first dc. (8)
Rnds 2–6: With brown, ch2, dc1 in each stitch around, sl st in first dc. (8) You can cut the black yarn.

Cut a long tail to attach tail later.

EYES (MAKE 2)

See photo tutorial on next page.

Rnd 1: With black, start with a magic loop, 6sc in the loop. (6)
Rnd 2: With white, sc2 in each of the next 3 stitches; continue with brown, sc2 in each of the next 3 stitches, sl st in first sc. Cut the black yarn, and cut a long piece of white yarn.
Rnd 3: Turn, skip the previous sc, *sc1 in next, 2sc in next stitch*, repeat from * to * one more time, sc1, sl st 1 in next, cut a long tail to sew the eye to the head later (you haven't used all stitches this rnd).

You'll fold rnd 3 of the eyelid over the eye and won't sew in it. You'll sew the brown part of rnd 2 with the remaining brown yarn and the white part of the eye with the white yarn. Sew to the head in rnds 13–15 on both sides of the head with 4 stitches in between. I always advise to pin in place first before sewing.

MAKING THE EYES

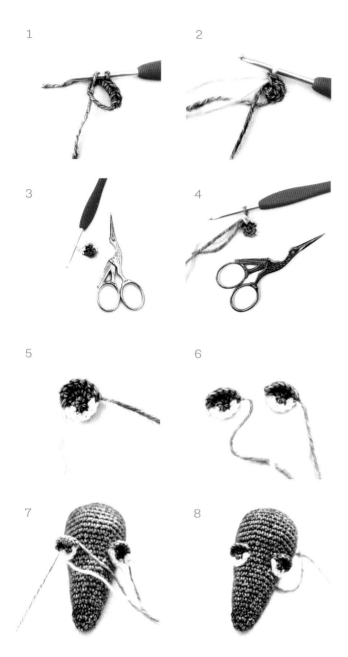

1
2
3
4
5
6
7
8

PUTTING IT ALL TOGETHER

- Take the body and place both legs between the bottom two layers. With the remaining yarn from the body, sew across the seam with the legs in between. This way you close the bottom and assemble pieces at the same time.
- Sew the tail on the back in the center of the body between rnds 16 and 17.
- Sew an arm to each side of the body between rnds 2 and 4.
- Sew the ears on both sides of the head in rnd 25.
- Finally, sew rnd 20 of the head to rnd 1 of the body.

BABY DACHSHUND

SIZE: 5.5 in (14 cm) tall

MATERIALS

Yarn: DK #3 light weight yarn; shown in Scheepjes Stone Washed
- Beige (Boulder Opal 804): 109.5 yd (100 m)
- Tiny scraps of black and white

Crochet hook: US size D-3 (3 mm)

Other:
- Fiberfill stuffing
- Needle and scissors

HEAD

Rnd 1: With black, start with a magic loop, 6sc in the loop. (6)

Rnd 2: *Sc1, 2sc in next*, repeat around. (9)

Rnd 3: With beige (you can cut the black yarn), sc1 in each stitch around. (9)

Rnd 4: *Sc2, 2sc in next*, repeat around. (12)

Rnd 5: Sc1 in each stitch around. (12)

Rnd 6: *Sc3, 2sc in next*, repeat around. (15)

Rnd 7: Sc1 in each stitch around. (15)

Rnd 8: *Sc4, 2sc in next*, repeat around. (18)

Rnd 9: Sc1 in each stitch around. (18)

Rnd 10: *Sc2, 2sc in next*, repeat around. (24)

Rnd 11: Sc1 in each stitch around. (24)

Rnd 12: *Sc3, 2sc in next*, repeat around. (30)

Rnds 13–15: Sc1 in each stitch around. (30)

Rnd 16: *Sc3, sc2tog*, repeat around. (24)

Rnd 17: *Sc2, sc2tog*, repeat around. (18) Stuff the head firmly and without any bumps.

Rnd 18: *Sc1, sc2tog*, repeat around. (12)

Rnd 19: *Sc2tog*, repeat around. (6) Cut a long tail, weave through the 6 remaining stitches, pull tight, and leave the end to sew the head to the body later.

EARS (MAKE 2)

Rnd 1: With beige, start with a magic loop, ch2 (doesn't count as first stitch now and throughout), 9dc in the loop, sl st in first dc. (9)
Rnd 2: Ch2, dc1 in each stitch around, sl st in first dc. (9)
Rnd 3: Ch2, *dc1, dc2tog*, repeat around, sl st in first dc. (6)

Cut a long tail to attach ears later.

BODY

Rnd 1: With beige, ch9, dc1 in 3rd ch from hook, dc5, 3dc in last, continue in the other side of the chains, dc6, 3dc in last, sl st in first dc. (18)
Rnd 2: Ch2 (doesn't count as first stitch now and throughout), *dc8, 2dc in next*, repeat one more time, sl st in first dc. (20)
Rnd 3: Ch2, *dc9, 2dc in next*, repeat one more time, sl st in first dc. (22)
Rnd 4: Ch2, *dc10, 2dc in next*, repeat one more time, sl st in first dc. (24)
Rnd 5: Ch2, *dc11, 2dc in next*, repeat one more time, sl st in first dc. (26)
Rnd 6: Ch2, *dc12, 2dc in next*, repeat one more time, sl st in first dc. (28)
Rnd 7: Ch2, *dc13, 2dc in next*, repeat one more time, sl st in first dc. (30)
Rnd 8: Ch2, *dc14, 2dc in next*, repeat one more time, sl st in first dc. (32)
Rnd 9: Ch2, *dc15, 2dc in next*, repeat one more time, sl st in first dc. (34)
Rnd 10: Ch2, *dc16, 2dc in next*, repeat one more time, sl st in first dc. (36)
Rnd 11: Ch2, *dc17, 2dc in next*, repeat one more time, sl st in first dc. (38)
Rnd 12: Ch2, *dc18, ch14, dc1 in 3rd ch from hook, dc1 in each of the remaining 11 chains, 2dc in next dc of rnd 11*, repeat one more time, sl st in first dc.

Cut a long tail to close the body later. Fold the body in line with the increases to make the belly straight.

ARMS (MAKE 2)

Rnd 1: With beige, start with a magic loop, 6sc in the loop. (6)
Rnd 2: 2sc in each stitch around. (12)
Rnds 3–5: Sc1 in each stitch around. (12)
Rnd 6: *Sc2, sc2tog*, repeat around. (9)
Rnd 7: Sl st 1, ch2 (doesn't count as first stitch now and throughout), dc1 in each stitch around, sl st in first dc. (9)
Rnd 8: Ch2, dc2tog, dc1 in each stitch around, sl st in first dc. (8)
Rnd 9: Ch2, dc1 in each stitch around, sl st in first dc. (8) Cut a long tail to attach arms later.

TAIL

Repeat instructions for ears. Cut a long tail to attach tail later.

EYES (MAKE 2)

Rnd 1: With black, start with a magic loop, 3sc in the loop; with white (you can cut the black yarn), 3sc in the loop. (6)
Rnd 2: With beige (you can cut a long tail of the white yarn to use later), 2sc in each of the next 3 stitches; cut a long beige tail to use later (you haven't used all the stitches in this rnd).

Pin and sew the eyes onto both sides of the head in rnds 9–11, 3 stitches apart.

TIP

The patterns for the dachshunds are ideal for using up leftovers. For example, make a striped body, or crochet the top of the body and the arms in a different color for a dachshund with a sweater on.

PUTTING IT ALL TOGETHER

- Fold the body in line with the increases to make the belly straight and sew closed with the remaining yarn. Tie a knot in the corners to form the feet.
- Sew the tail on the back in the center of the body in rnd 9.
- Sew an arm to each side of the body between rnds 2 and 3.
- Sew the ears on both sides of the head in rnd 15.
- Finally, sew the bottom of rnd 10 of the head to rnd 1 of the body.

PIG

DIFFICULTY LEVEL: 3 of 5

SIZE: 10 in (25 cm) tall

MATERIALS

Yarn: DK #3 light weight yarn; shown in Scheepjes Stone Washed
- Pink (Rose Quartz): 164 yd (150 m)
- Gray (Smokey Quartz 802): 76.5 yd (70 m)

Crochet hook: US size D-3 (3 mm)

Other:
- Black safety eyes, 15 mm
- Fiberfill stuffing
- Needle and scissors

NOSE

Rnd 1: With pink, ch5, 4sc in 2nd ch from hook, sc2, 4sc in next ch; now continue in the other side of the chains, sc4. (14)

Rnd 2: *2sc in each of the next 3 sc, sc4*, repeat from * to * one more time. (20)

Rnd 3: In back loops only, sc1 in each stitch around. (20)

Rnds 4–6: Sc1 in each stitch around. (20)

Cut a long tail to sew onto head later.

Nose

EARS (MAKE 2, 1 IN PINK AND 1 IN GRAY)

Rnd 1: Start with a magic loop, ch2 (doesn't count as first dc now and throughout), 6dc in the loop, sl st in first dc. (6)

Rnd 2: Ch2, dc3, 2dc in each of the next 3 dc, sl st in first dc. (9)

Rnd 3: Ch2, dc3, 2dc in each of the next 6 dc, sl st in first dc. (15)

Rnds 4–5: Ch2, dc1 in each stitch around, sl st in first dc. (15)

Cut a long tail to sew onto head later.

EYE SPOT

Rnd 1: With gray, start with a magic loop, 3sc in the loop, ch1, 6dc in the loop. (9)

Don't make the magic loop too tight; you'll insert the safety eye later.

Rnd 2: 2sc in each of the next 3 sc, ch1, 2dc in each of the next 4 dc, ch2, sl st in next dc; you'll leave the last dc unworked.

Cut a long tail to sew onto head later.

HEAD

Rnd 1: With pink, start with a magic loop, 6sc in the loop. (6)

Rnd 2: 2sc in each stitch around. (12)

Rnd 3: *Sc1, 2sc in next stitch*, repeat around. (18)

Rnd 4: *Sc2, 2sc in next stitch*, repeat around. (24)

Rnd 5: *Sc3, 2sc in next stitch*, repeat around. (30)

Rnd 6: *Sc4, 2sc in next stitch*, repeat around. (36)

Rnd 7: *Sc5, 2sc in next stitch*, repeat around. (42)

Rnd 8: *Sc6, 2sc in next stitch*, repeat around. (48)

Rnd 9: *Sc7, 2sc in next stitch*, repeat around. (54)

Rnds 10–20: Sc1 in each stitch around. (54)

Rnd 21: *Sc7, sc2tog*, repeat around. (48)

Rnd 22: *Sc6, sc2tog*, repeat around. (42)

Rnd 23: *Sc5, sc2tog*, repeat around. (36)

Rnd 24: *Sc4, sc2tog*, repeat around. (30)

Rnd 25: *Sc3, sc2tog*, repeat around. (24)

Rnd 26: *Sc2, sc2tog*, repeat around. (18)

Stuff the nose lightly, and pin and sew in place. The nose is centered on the face over rnds 15–21.

Take the eye spot, insert the safety eye into the center of the eye spot, and place it on the left side of the face over rnds 11–18. Attach back of the safety eye on the inside of the head and sew the eye spot in place. Insert the other safety eye at the same height with ±11 stitches in between the patch and the eye.

Stuff the head neatly.

Rnd 27: *Sc1, sc2tog*, repeat around. (12)

Rnd 28: *Sc2tog*, repeat around (6)

Cut a long tail, weave through the 6 remaining stitches, pull tight, and leave the end to sew the head to the body later. Sew ears to both sides of the head over rnds 9–15.

BODY

Rnd 1: With pink, ch18, 1dc in 3rd ch from hook, dc14, 3dc in last, continue along the other side of the chains, dc15, 3dc in last, sl st in first dc. (36)

Rnd 2: Ch2 (doesn't count as first stitch now and throughout), *dc17, 2dc in next*, repeat one more time, sl st in first dc. (38)

Rnd 3: Ch2, *dc18, 2dc in next*, repeat one more time, sl st in first dc. (40)

Rnd 4: Ch2, *dc19, 2dc in next*, repeat one more time, sl st in first dc. (42)

Rnd 5: Ch2, *dc20, 2dc in next*, repeat one more time, sl st in first dc. (44)

Rnd 6: Ch2, *dc21, 2dc in next*, repeat one more time, sl st in first dc. (46)

Rnd 7: Ch2, *dc22, 2dc in next*, repeat one more time, sl st in first dc. (48)

Rnd 8: Ch2, *dc23, 2dc in next*, repeat one more time, sl st in first dc. (50)

Rnd 9: Ch2, *dc24, 2dc in next*, repeat one more time, sl st in first dc. (52)

Rnd 10: Ch2, *dc25, 2dc in next*, repeat one more time, sl st in first dc. (54)

Rnd 11: Ch2, *dc26, 2dc in next*, repeat one more time, sl st in first dc. (56)

Rnd 12: Ch2, *dc12, dc2tog*, repeat around, sl st in first dc. (52)

Rnd 13: Ch2, dc5, dc2tog, *dc11, dc2tog*, repeat 2 more times, dc6, sl st in first dc. (48)

Rnd 14: Ch2, *dc10, dc2tog*, repeat around, sl st in first dc. (44)

Rnd 15: Ch2, dc4, dc2tog, *dc9, dc2tog*, repeat 2 more times, dc5, sl st in first dc. (40)

Rnd 16: Ch2, *dc8, dc2tog*, repeat around, sl st in first dc. (36)

Rnd 17: Ch2, dc3, dc2tog, *dc7, dc2tog*, repeat 2 more times, dc4, sl st in first dc. (32)

Rnd 18: Ch2, *dc6, dc2tog*, repeat around, sl st in first dc. (28)

Cut a long tail to close the body later. Fold the body in line with the increases to make the belly straight.

TAIL

Rnd 1: With pink, ch20, 3sc in 2nd ch from hook, 3sc in each chain to end. (57)

Cut a long tail to sew to body later.

ARMS (MAKE 2)

Rnd 1: With gray, start with a magic loop, 6sc in the loop. (6)

Rnd 2: 2sc in each stitch around. (12)

Rnd 3: *Sc1, 2sc in next stitch*, repeat around. (18)

Rnds 4–6: Sc1 in each stitch around. (18)

Rnd 7: *Sc4, sc2tog*, repeat around. (15)

Rnds 8–9: Sc1 in each stitch around. (15)

Rnd 10: With pink (cut an extra-long gray tail to use later), sl st 1, ch2 (doesn't count as first dc now and throughout), dc1 in each stitch around, sl st in first dc. (15)

Rnd 11: Ch2, dc2tog, dc1 in each stitch around, sl st in first dc. (14)

Rnd 12: Ch2, dc1 in each stitch around, sl st in first dc. (14)

Rnd 13: Ch2, dc2tog, dc1 in each stitch around, sl st in first dc. (13)

Rnd 14: Ch2, dc1 in each stitch around, sl st in first dc. (13)

Cut a long tail to attach arms later.

LEGS (MAKE 2)

Repeat instructions for arm from rnds 1 to 12.

Cut yarn and weave in ends.

MAKING THE PERFECT PIGGYTOES
(instructions for both legs and arms)

1. Stuff the hoof lightly and sew closed between rnds 9 and 10.
2. Bring your yarn to the center of rnd 9.
3. Insert needle into rnd 1.
4. Insert needle back to center at same point as step 2.
5. Pull tight and repeat steps 3–5 once more.
6. Repeat steps 2–5 for the back of the hoof.
7. Weave in ends and cut yarn.

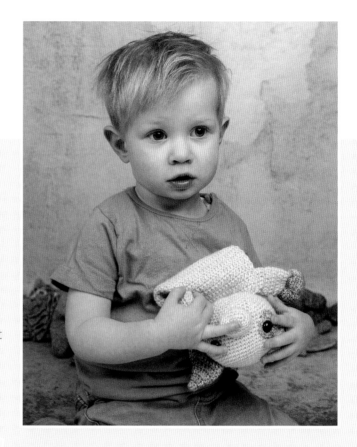

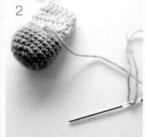

PUTTING IT ALL TOGETHER

- Take the body and place both legs between the bottom two layers. With the remaining yarn from the body, sew across the seam with the legs in between. This way you close the bottom and assemble pieces at the same time.
- Sew the tail on the back in the center of the body in rnd 17.
- Sew an arm to each side of the body between rnds 2 and 4.
- Finally, sew rnd 22 of the head to rnd 1 of the body.

BABY PIG

DIFFICULTY LEVEL: 3 of 5

SIZE: 6 in (15 cm) tall

MATERIALS

Yarn: DK #3 light weight yarn; shown in Scheepjes Stone Washed
- Pink (Rose Quartz): 120.5 yd (110 m)
- Gray (Smokey Quartz 802): 54.5 yd (50 m)

Crochet hook: US size D-3 (3 mm)

Other:
- Black safety eyes, 10 mm
- Fiberfill stuffing
- Needle and scissors

NOSE

Rnd 1: With pink, ch5, 4sc in 2nd ch from hook, sc2, 4sc in next ch, now continue in the other side of the chains, sc4. (14)

Rnd 2: In back loops only, sc1 in each stitch around. (14)

Rnd 3: Sc1 in each stitch around. (14)

Cut a long tail to sew onto head later.

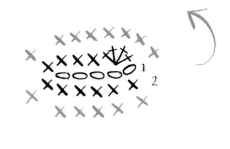

Nose

EYE SPOT

Rnd 1: With gray, start with a magic loop, 3sc in the loop, ch1, 6dc in the loop, sl st in first sc. (9) Don't make the magic loop too tight; you'll insert the safety eye later.

Cut a long tail to sew onto head later.

HEAD

Rnd 1: With pink, start with a magic loop, 6sc in the loop. (6)
Rnd 2: 2sc in each stitch around. (12)
Rnd 3: *Sc1, 2sc in next stitch*, repeat around. (18)
Rnd 4: *Sc2, 2sc in next stitch*, repeat around. (24)
Rnd 5: *Sc3, 2sc in next stitch*, repeat around. (30)
Rnd 6: *Sc4, 2sc in next stitch*, repeat around. (36)
Rnds 7–13: Sc1 in each stitch around. (36)
Rnd 14: *Sc4, sc2tog*, repeat around. (30)
Rnd 15: *Sc3, sc2tog*, repeat around. (24)
Rnd 16: *Sc2, sc2tog*, repeat around. (18)

Stuff the nose lightly, and pin and sew in place. The nose is centered on the face over rnds 10–13.

Take the eye spot, insert the safety eye into the center of the eye spot, and place it on the right side of the face over rnds 9–12. Attach back of the safety eye on the inside of the head and sew the eye spot in place. Insert the other safety eye at the same height with ±7 stitches in between the patch and the eye.

Stuff the head neatly.

Rnd 17: *Sc1, sc2tog*, repeat around. (12)
Rnd 18: *Sc2tog*, repeat around. (6)

Cut a long tail, weave through the 6 remaining stitches, pull tight, and leave the end to sew the head to the body later.

EARS (MAKE 2, 1 IN PINK AND 1 IN GRAY)

Rnd 1: Start with a magic loop, ch2 (doesn't count as first dc now and throughout), 6dc in the loop, sl st in first dc. (6)
Rnd 2: Ch2, *dc1, 2dc in next stitch*, repeat around, sl st in first dc. (9)
Rnd 3: Ch2, *dc2, 2dc in next stitch*, sl st in first dc. (12)
Rnd 4: Ch2, dc1 in each stitch around, sl st in first dc. (12)

Cut a long tail and sew ears to both sides of the head over rnds 5–9.

BODY

Rnd 1: With pink, ch13, dc1 in 3rd ch from hook, dc9, 3dc in last, continue along the other side of the chains, dc10, 3dc in last, sl st in first dc. (26)
Rnd 2: Ch2 (doesn't count as first stitch now and throughout), *dc12, 2dc in next*, repeat one more time, sl st in first dc. (28)
Rnd 3: Ch2, *dc13, 2dc in next*, repeat one more time, sl st in first dc. (30)
Rnd 4: Ch2, *dc14, 2dc in next*, repeat one more time, sl st in first dc. (32)
Rnd 5: Ch2, *dc15, 2dc in next*, repeat one more time, sl st in first dc. (34)
Rnd 6: Ch2, *dc16, 2dc in next*, repeat one more time, sl st in first dc. (36)
Rnd 7: Ch2, *dc17, 2dc in next*, repeat one more time, sl st in first dc. (38)
Rnd 8: Ch2, *dc18, 2dc in next*, repeat one more time, sl st in first dc. (40)
Rnd 9: Ch2, *dc8, dc2tog*, repeat around, sl st in first dc. (36)
Rnd 10: Ch2, dc3, dc2tog, *dc7, dc2tog*, repeat 2 more times, dc4, sl st in first dc. (32)
Rnd 11: Ch2, *dc6, dc2tog*, repeat around, sl st in first dc. (28)

Rnd 12: Ch2, *with pink: dc2, dc2tog, dc5, dc2tog, dc3, with gray: ch14, dc1 in 3rd ch from hook, dc1 in each of the remaining 11 chains*, repeat one more time, sl st in first dc.

Cut a long tail to close the body later.

TAIL

Rnd 1: With pink, ch15, 3sc in 2nd ch from hook, 3sc in each chain to end. (42)

Cut a long tail to sew to body later.

ARMS (MAKE 2)

Rnd 1: With gray, start with a magic loop, 6sc in the loop. (6)
Rnd 2: 2sc in each stitch around. (12)

Rnd 3: *Sc1, 2sc in next*, repeat around. (18)
Rnds 4–5: Sc in each stitch around. (18)
Rnd 6: *Sc1, sc2tog*, repeat around. (12)
Rnd 7: Sc1 in each stitch around. (12) Cut a long tail; you'll use it later.
Rnd 8: With pink, sl st 1, ch2 (doesn't count as first stitch now and throughout), dc1 in each stitch around, sl st in first dc. (12)
Rnd 9: Ch2, dc2tog, dc1 in each stitch around, sl st in first dc. (11)
Rnd 10: Ch2, dc1 in each stitch around, sl st in first dc. (11)
Rnd 11: Ch2, dc2tog, dc1 in each stitch around, sl st in first dc. (10)
Rnd 12: Ch2, dc1 in each stitch around, sl st in first dc. (10)

Cut a long tail to attach arms to body later.

Note: To make the perfect pig's hooves, see the tutorial on page 40.

PUTTING IT ALL TOGETHER

- Fold the body in line with the increases to make the belly straight and sew closed with the remaining yarn. Tie a knot in the corners to form the feet.
- Sew the tail on the back in the center of the body in rnd 10.
- Sew an arm to each side of the body between rnds 1 and 2.
- Attach an ear on each side of the head between rnds 5 and 10.
- Finally, sew rnd 14 of the head to rnd 1 of the body.

HEDGEHOG

DIFFICULTY LEVEL: 4 of 5

✗ ✗ ✗ ✗ ✕

SIZE: 7 in (18 cm) tall

MATERIALS

Yarn: DK #3 light weight yarn; shown in Scheepjes Stone Washed
- Brown (Brown Agate 822): 131 yd (120 m)
- Light pink (Pink Quartz-ite 821): 109.5 yd (100 m)
- Black (Black Onyx 803): 22 yd (20 m)

Crochet hook: US size D-3 (3 mm)

Other:
- Fiberfill stuffing
- Needle and scissors

HEAD

Rnd 1: With black, start with a magic loop, 6sc in the loop. (6)

Rnd 2: 2sc in each stitch around. (12)

Rnds 3–4: Sc1 in each stitch around. (12)

Rnd 5: Continue with light pink (you can cut the black yarn), sc6, 2sc in each of the next 6 stitches. (18)

Rnds 6–7: Sc1 in each stitch around. (18)

Rnd 8: Sc6, *sc1, 2sc in next*, repeat around. (24)

Rnd 9: Sc1 in each stitch around. (24)

Rnd 10: Sc6, *sc2, 2sc in next*, repeat around. (30)

Rnd 11: Sc1 in each stitch around. (30)

Rnd 12: Sc6, *sc3, 2sc in next*, repeat around. (36)

Rnd 13: Sc6, *sc4, 2sc in next*, repeat around. (42)

Rnd 14: Sc6, *sc5, 2sc in next*, repeat around. (48)

Rnd 15: Continue with brown (you can cut the light pink yarn), in back loops only, sc1 in each stitch around. (48)

Rnd 16: Sc1 in each stitch around. (48)

Rnd 17: In back loops only, sc1 in each stitch around. (48)

Rnd 18: *Sc6, sc2tog*, repeat around. (42)

Rnd 19: In back loops only, *sc5, sc2tog*, repeat around. (36)

Rnd 20: *Sc4, sc2tog*, repeat around. (30)

Rnd 21: In back loops only, *sc3, sc2tog*, repeat around. (24)

Rnd 22: *Sc2, sc2tog*, repeat around. (18)

Stuff the head.

Rnd 23: In back loops only, *sc1, sc2tog*, repeat around. (12)

Rnd 24: *Sc2tog*, repeat around. (6)

Cut a long tail, weave through the 6 remaining stitches, pull tight, and leave the end to sew the head to the body later.

SPINES (HEAD)

Rnd 1: Attach the brown yarn in the first unworked front loop of rnd 14, with the nose facing you, *sc1, skip 1, (in next stitch: 1dc, ch3, sl st in first of the 3 chains you just made and 1dc), skip 1*, repeat from * to * along all of the unworked loops around the entire head.

Cut yarn and weave in ends.

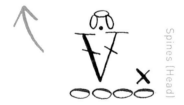

Spines (Head)

EARS (MAKE 2)

Rnd 1: With light pink, start with a magic loop, ch2 (doesn't count as first stitch now and throughout), 6dc in the loop, sl st in first dc. (6)

Rnd 2: Ch2, *dc1, 2dc in next*, repeat around, sl st in first dc. (9)

Cut a long tail to attach ears later.

EYES (MAKE 2)

Rnd 1: With black, start with a magic loop, 6sc in the loop, sl st in first sc. (6)

Cut a long tail to attach eyes later.

BODY

Rnd 1: With light pink, ch9, 5dc in 3rd ch from hook, dc5, 5dc in last, continue along the other side of the chains, dc5, sl st in first dc. (20)

Rnd 2: Ch2 (doesn't count as first stitch now and throughout), *2dc in each of the next 5 stitches, dc5*, repeat from * to * one more time, sl st in first dc. (30)

Rnd 3: Ch2, ^*dc1, 2dc in next*, repeat from * to * 4 more times, dc5^, repeat from ^ to ^ one more time, sl st in first dc. (40)

Rnd 4: Ch2, ^*dc2, 2dc in next*, repeat from * to * 4 more times, dc5^, repeat from ^ to ^ one more time, sl st in first dc. (50)

Rnd 5: Ch2, ^*dc3, 2dc in next*, repeat from * to * 4 more times, dc5^, repeat from ^ to ^ one more time, sl st in first dc. (60)

Rnd 6: Ch2, ^*dc4, 2dc in next*, repeat from * to * 4 more times, dc5^, repeat from ^ to ^ one more time, sl st in first dc. (70)

From now on, you'll work all rnds in back loops only.

Rnd 7: With brown (you can cut the light pink yarn), ch2, ^*dc5, 2dc in next*, repeat from * to * 4 more times, dc5^, repeat from ^ to ^ one more time, sl st in first dc. (80)

Rnd 8: Ch2, ^*dc5, dc2tog*, repeat from * to * 4 more times, dc5^, repeat from ^ to ^ one more time, sl st in first dc. (70)

Rnd 9: Ch2, ^*dc4, dc2tog*, repeat from * to * 4 more times, dc5^, repeat from ^ to ^ one more time, sl st in first dc. (60)

Rnd 10: Ch2, ^*dc3, dc2tog*, repeat from * to * 4 more times, dc5^, repeat from ^ to ^ one more time, sl st in first dc. (50)

Rnd 11: Ch2, ^*dc2, dc2tog*, repeat from * to * 4 more times, dc5^, repeat from ^ to ^ one more time, sl st in first dc. (40)

Rnd 12: Ch2, ^*dc1, dc2tog*, repeat from * to * 4 more times, dc5^, repeat from ^ to ^ one more time, sl st in first dc. (30)

Rnd 13: Ch2, ^*dc2tog*, repeat from * to * 4 more times, dc5^, repeat from ^ to ^ one more time, sl st in first dc. (20)

Rnd 14: Ch2, *dc4tog*, repeat around, sl st in first dc. (5)

Cut a long tail, weave through the 5 remaining stitches, pull tight, and weave in ends.

SPINES (BODY)

Rnd 1: Attach the brown yarn in the first un-worked front loop of rnd 6 and work in the same direction as the rest of the body, *sc1, skip 2, (in next stitch: 3dc, ch3, sl st in first of the 3 chains you just made, 3dc), skip 2, sc1, skip 1, (in next stitch: dc1, ch3, sl st in first of the 3 chains you just made, dc1), skip 1*, repeat from * to * around, sl st in first sc.

Rnd 2: Now continue in the first unworked front loop of rnd 7, *sc1, skip 1, (in next stitch: dc1, ch3, sl st in first of the 3 chains you just made, dc1), skip 1, sc1, skip 2, (in next stitch: 3dc, ch3, sl st in first of the 3 chains you just made, 3dc), skip 2*, repeat from * to * around.

Rnd 3: Now continue in the first unworked front loop of rnd 8, *sc1, skip 2, (in next stitch: 3dc, ch3, sl st in first of the 3 chains you just made, 3dc), skip 2, sc1, skip 1, (in next stitch: dc1, ch3, sl st in first of the 3 chains you just made, dc1), skip 1*, repeat from * to * around, sl st in first sc.

Repeat rnds 2 and 3 until you've worked all rnds, cut the yarn, and weave in ends.

ARMS (MAKE 2)

Rnd 1: With light pink, start with a magic loop, 6sc in the loop. (6)

Rnd 2: 2sc in each stitch around. (12)

Rnd 3: *Sc1, 2sc in next stitch*, repeat around. (18)

Rnds 4–6: Sc1 in each stitch around. (18)

Rnd 7: *Sc4, sc2tog*, repeat around. (15)

Rnds 8–9: Sc1 in each stitch around. (15)

Rnd 10: Sl st 1, ch2 (doesn't count as first stitch now and throughout), dc1 in each stitch around, sl st in first dc. (15)

Rnd 11: Ch2, dc2tog, dc1 in each stitch around, sl st in first dc. (14)

Rnd 12: Ch2, dc1 in each stitch around, sl st in first dc. (14)

Rnd 13: Ch2, dc2tog, dc1 in each stitch around, sl st in first dc. (13)

Cut a long tail to attach arms later.

LEGS (MAKE 2)

Rnd 1: With light pink, start with a magic loop, ch2 (doesn't count as first stitch now and throughout), dc12 in the loop, sl st in first dc. (12)

Rnds 2–5: Ch2, dc1 in each stitch around, sl st in first dc. (12)

Cut a long tail to attach legs later.

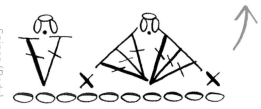

PUTTING IT ALL TOGETHER

- Sew the arms to each side of the upper body in rnd 6.
- Sew the legs to each side of the lower body in in rnd 6.
- Pin and sew the ears on top of both sides of the head in rnd 14.
- Pin and sew the eyes between rnds 8 and 10, 7 stitches apart.
- Finally, sew the bottom of rnd 18 of the head to rnd 7 of the body.

BABY HEDGEHOG

DIFFICULTY LEVEL: 4 of 5

SIZE: 4.5 in (12 cm) tall

MATERIALS

Yarn: DK #3 light weight yarn; shown in Scheepjes Stone Washed
- Brown (Brown Agate 822): 87.5 yd (80 m)
- Light pink (Pink Quartz-ite 821): 76.5 yd (70 m)
- Black (Black Onyx 803): 11 yd (10 m)

Crochet hook: US size D-3 (3 mm)

Other:
- Fiberfill stuffing
- Needle and scissors

HEAD

Rnd 1: With black, start with a magic loop, 6sc in the loop. (6)

Rnd 2: *Sc2, 2sc in next*, repeat around. (8)

Rnd 3: Continue with light pink (you can cut the black yarn), *sc3, 2sc in next*, repeat around. (10)

Rnd 4: Sc1 in each stitch around. (10)

Rnd 5: *Sc4, 2sc in next*, repeat around. (12)

Rnd 6: Sc6, 2sc in each of the next 6 stitches. (18)

Rnd 7: Sc1 in each stitch around. (18)

Rnd 8: Sc6, *sc1, 2sc in next*, repeat around. (24)

Rnd 9: Sc1 in each stitch around. (24)

Rnd 10: Sc6, *sc2, 2sc in next*, repeat around. (30)

Rnd 11: Continue with brown (you can cut the light pink yarn), in back loops only, sc1 in each stitch around. (30)

Rnd 12: Sc1 in each stitch around. (30)

Rnd 13: In back loops only, *sc3, sc2tog*, repeat around. (24)

Rnd 14: *Sc2, sc2tog*, repeat around. (18)

Stuff the head.

Rnd 15: In back loops only, *sc1, sc2tog*, repeat around. (12)

Rnd 16: *Sc2tog*, repeat around. (6)

Cut a long tail, weave through the 6 remaining stitches, pull tight, and leave the end to sew the head to the body later.

SPINES (HEAD)

Rnd 1: Attach the brown yarn in the first un-worked front loop of rnd 10, with the nose facing you, *sc1, skip 1, (in next stitch: 1dc, ch3, sl st in first of the 3 chains you just made and 1dc), skip 1*, repeat from * to * along all of the unworked loops around the entire head.

Cut yarn and weave in ends.

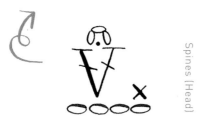

Spines (Head)

EARS (MAKE 2)

Rnd 1: With light pink, start with a magic loop, ch2 (doesn't count as first stitch now and throughout), 6dc in the loop, sl st in first dc. (6)

Cut a long tail to attach ears later.

BODY

Rnd 1: With light pink, ch9, 5dc in 3rd ch from hook, dc5, 5dc in last, continue along the other side of the chains, dc5, sl st in first dc. (20)

Rnd 2: Ch2 (doesn't count as first stitch now and throughout), *2dc in each of the next 5 stitch-es, dc5*, repeat from * to * one more time, sl st in first dc. (30)

Rnd 3: Ch2, ^*dc1, 2dc in next*, repeat from * to * 4 more times, dc5^, repeat from ^ to ^ one more time, sl st in first dc. (40)

From now on, work all rnds in back loops only.

Rnd 4: With brown (you can cut the light pink yarn), ch2, ^*dc2, 2dc in next*, repeat from * to

* 4 more times, dc5^, repeat from ^ to ^ one more time, sl st in first dc. (50)

Rnd 5: Ch2, ^*dc2, dc2tog*, repeat from * to * 4 more times, dc5^, repeat from ^ to ^ one more time, sl st in first dc. (40)

Rnd 6: Ch2, ^*dc1, dc2tog*, repeat from * to * 4 more times, dc5^, repeat from ^ to ^ one more time, sl st in first dc. (30)

Rnd 7: Ch2, ^*dc2tog*, repeat from * to * 4 more times, dc5^, repeat from ^ to ^ one more time, sl st in first dc. (20)

Rnd 8: Ch2, *dc4tog*, repeat around, sl st in first dc. (5)

Cut a long tail, weave through the 5 remaining stitches, pull tight, and weave in ends.

SPINES (BODY)

Rnd 1: Attach the brown yarn in the first un-worked front loop of rnd 3, *sc1, skip 2, (in next stitch: 3dc, ch3, sl st in first of the 3 chains you just made, 3dc), skip 2, sc1, skip 1, (in next stitch: dc1, ch3, sl st in first of the 3 chains you just made, dc1), skip 1*, repeat from * to * around, sl st in first sc.

Rnd 2: Now continue in the first unworked front loop of rnd 4, *sc1, skip 1, (in next stitch: dc1, ch3, sl st in first of the 3 chains you just made, dc1), skip 1, sc1, skip 2, (in next stitch: 3dc, ch3, sl st in first of the 3 chains you just made, 3dc), skip 2*, repeat from * to * around.

Rnd 3: Now continue in the first unworked front loop of rnd 5, *sc1, skip 2, (in next stitch: 3dc, ch3, sl st in first of the 3 chains you just made, 3dc), skip 2, sc1, skip 1, (in next stitch: dc1, ch3, sl st in first of the 3 chains you just made, dc1), skip 1*, repeat from * to * around, sl st in first sc.

Repeat rnds 2 and 3 until you've worked all rnds, cut the yarn, and weave in ends.

ARMS (MAKE 2)

Rnd 1: With light pink, start with a magic loop, 6sc in the loop. (6)

Rnd 2: 2sc in each stitch around. (12)

Rnds 3–5: Sc1 in each stitch around. (12)

Rnd 6: *Sc2, sc2tog*, repeat around. (9)

Rnd 7: Sl st 1, ch2 (doesn't count as first stitch now and throughout), dc1 in each stitch around, sl st in first dc. (9)

Rnd 8: Ch2, dc2tog, dc1 in each stitch around, sl st in first dc. (8)

Rnd 9: Ch2, dc1 in each stitch around, sl st in first dc. (8)

Cut a long tail to attach arms later.

LEGS (MAKE 2)

Rnd 1: With light pink, start with a magic loop, ch2 (doesn't count as first stitch now and throughout), dc6 in the loop, sl st in first dc. (6)

Rnd 2: Ch2, dc1 in each stitch around, sl st in first dc. (6)

Cut a long tail to attach legs later.

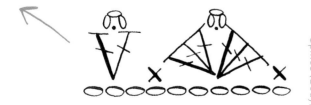

Spines (Body)

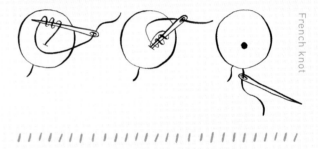

French knot

PUTTING IT ALL TOGETHER

- Sew the arms to each side of the upper body in rnd 3.
- Sew the legs to each side of the lower body in rnd 3.
- Pin and sew the ears on top of both sides of the head in rnd 10.
- Sew the bottom of rnd 11 of the head to rnd 4 of the body.
- Finally, embroider the eyes on each side of the head between rnds 6 and 7, 5 stitches apart, by making a French knot.

SLEEPY BEAR

DIFFICULTY LEVEL: 3 of 5

SIZE: 10 in (25 cm) tall, excluding cap

MATERIALS

Yarn: DK #3 light weight yarn; shown in Scheepjes Stone Washed
- Brown (Boulder Opal 804): 87.5 yd (80 m)
- Blue (Amazonite 813) or pink (Rose Quartz 820): 87.5 yd (80 m)
- White (Moon Stone 801): 87.5 yd (80 m)
- Black (Black Onyx 803): 22 yd (20 m)

Crochet hook: US size D-3 (3 mm)

Other:
- Fiberfill stuffing
- Needle and scissors

Note: The pattern is described for the blue bear. If you want to make a pink variant, replace the instructions for blue with pink everywhere.

HEAD

Rnd 1: With brown, start with a magic loop, 6sc in the loop. (6)
Rnd 2: 2sc in each stitch around. (12)
Rnd 3: *Sc1, 2sc in next stitch*, repeat around. (18)
Rnd 4: *Sc2, 2sc in next stitch*, repeat around. (24)
Rnd 5: *Sc3, 2sc in next stitch*, repeat around. (30)
Rnd 6: *Sc4, 2sc in next stitch*, repeat around. (36)
Rnd 7: *Sc5, 2sc in next stitch*, repeat around. (42)
Rnd 8: *Sc6, 2sc in next stitch*, repeat around. (48)
Rnds 9–18: Sc1 in each stitch around. (48)
Rnd 19: *Sc6, sc2tog*, repeat around. (42)
Rnd 20: *Sc5, sc2tog*, repeat around. (36)
Rnd 21: *Sc4, sc2tog*, repeat around. (30)
Rnd 22: *Sc3, sc2tog*, repeat around. (24)
Rnd 23: *Sc2, sc2tog*, repeat around. (18)

Stuff the head neatly.

Rnd 24: *Sc1, sc2tog*, repeat around. (12)
Rnd 25: *Sc2tog*, repeat around. (6)

Cut a long tail, weave through the 6 remaining stitches, pull tight, and weave in ends.

EYES (MAKE 2)

Rnd 1: With black, start with a magic loop, 6sc in the loop, sl st in first sc, pull tight.

Cut a long tail to attach the eyes to the head later.

NOSE

Rnd 1: With black, start with a magic loop, 6sc in the loop. (6)
Rnd 2: 2sc in each of the next 4sc, continue with brown (you can cut the black yarn), 2sc in each of the next 2sc. (12)
Rnd 3: *Sc1, 2sc in next stitch*, repeat around. (18)
Rnd 4: *Sc2, 2sc in next stitch*, repeat around. (24)
Rnd 5: Sc1 in each stitch around. (24)

Cut a long tail to attach the nose to the head later.

EARS (MAKE 2)

Rnd 1: With brown, start with a magic loop, 6sc in the loop. (6)
Rnd 2: 2sc in each stitch around. (12)
Rnd 3: *Sc1, 2sc in next*, repeat around. (18)
Rnds 4–5: Sc1 in each stitch around. (18)

Cut a long tail to attach the ears to the head later.

BODY

When making the body, hat, and arms, you'll change colors a lot. You can leave the yarn you're not working with and just pick it up whenever you need it. Make sure to not pull the yarn too tight, to keep the fabric nice and relaxed.

Rnd 1: With blue (leave a long tail to use later), ch18, 1dc in 3rd ch from hook, dc14, 3dc in last, continue along the other side of the chains, dc15, 3dc in last, sl st in first dc. (36)
Rnd 2: With white, ch2 (doesn't count as first stitch now and throughout), *dc17, 2dc in next*, repeat one more time, sl st in first dc. (38)
Rnd 3: With blue, ch2, *dc18, 2dc in next*, repeat one more time, sl st in first dc. (40)
Rnd 4: With white, ch2, *dc19, 2dc in next*, repeat one more time, sl st in first dc. (42)
Rnd 5: With blue, ch2, *dc20, 2dc in next*, repeat one more time, sl st in first dc. (44)
Rnd 6: With white, ch2, *dc21, 2dc in next*, repeat one more time, sl st in first dc. (46)
Rnd 7: With blue, ch2, *dc22, 2dc in next*, repeat one more time, sl st in first dc. (48)
Rnd 8: With white, ch2, *dc23, 2dc in next*, repeat one more time, sl st in first dc. (50)
Rnd 9: With blue, ch2, *dc24, 2dc in next*, repeat one more time, sl st in first dc. (52)
Rnd 10: With white, ch2, *dc25, 2dc in next*, repeat one more time, sl st in first dc. (54)
Rnd 11: With blue, ch2, *dc26, 2dc in next*, repeat one more time, sl st in first dc. (56)
Rnd 12: With white, ch2, *dc27, 2dc in next*, repeat one more time, sl st in first dc. (58)
Rnd 13: With blue, ch2, dc1 in each stitch around, sl st in first dc. (58)
Rnd 14: With white, ch2, dc1 in each stitch around, sl st in first dc. (58)
Rnd 15: With blue, ch2, dc1 in each stitch around, sl st in first dc. (58)

Cut a long piece of yarn to close the body later.

FIRST LEG

Rnd 16: With white, ch2, dc10, skip 38 stitches (you'll continue with the leg on the back of the body), dc10, sl st in first dc. (20)
Rnd 17: With blue, ch2, dc1 in each stitch around, sl st in first dc. (20)

Rnd 18: With white, ch2, dc1 in each stitch around, sl st in first dc. (20)

Rnds 19–20: Repeat rnds 17–18.

You can cut the white and blue yarn and weave in ends now or later.

FOOT

Rnd 21: Attach the brown yarn in the back loop of the first stitch of rnd 20 (leave a long brown piece of yarn to use later). In back loops only, sc1 in each stitch around. (20)

Rnds 22–25: Sc1 in each stitch around. (20)

Rnd 26: *Sc3, sc2tog*, repeat around. (16)

Rnd 27: *Sc2, sc2tog*, repeat around. (12)

Rnd 28: *Sc1, sc2tog*, repeat around. (8)

Cut a long tail, weave through the 8 remaining stitches, pull tight, and weave in ends.

SECOND LEG

Rnd 16: Continue in rnd 15 (in which you also made the first leg), skip 9 stitches, attach the white yarn in the next stitch, ch2, dc20, sl st in first dc of this leg. (20)

Rnds 17–28: Repeat instructions of the first leg and foot.

Stuff both feet through the opening in between the legs and with the brown yarn (of rnd 21) sew each foot closed between rnds 20 and 21. Take a small piece of blue yarn and sew the opening in between the legs closed.

Optional flouncing edge (for girl bear): Attach the pink yarn in the first unworked front loop of leg or sleeve, crochet 3sc in each unworked front loop around, sl st in first sc, weave in ends.

ARMS (MAKE 2)

Rnd 1: With blue, leave a long tail to attach arms to body later, ch14, sl st in first ch to close the rnd (make sure the chains aren't twisted), ch2 (doesn't count as first stitch now and throughout), dc1 in each stitch around, sl st in first dc. (14)

Rnd 2: With white, ch2, 2dc in first dc, dc1 in each stitch around, sl st in first dc. (15)

Rnd 3: With blue, ch2, dc1 in each stitch around, sl st in first dc. (15)

Rnd 4: With white, ch2, 2dc in first dc, dc1 in each stitch around, sl st in first dc. (16)

Rnd 5: With blue, ch2, dc1 in each stitch around, sl st in first dc. (16)

Rnd 6: With white, ch2, 2dc in first dc, dc1 in each stitch around, sl st in first dc. (17)

Rnd 7: With blue, ch2, dc1 in each stitch around, sl st in first dc. (17)

Rnd 8: With white, ch2, 2dc in first dc, dc1 in each stitch around, sl st in first dc. (18)

You can cut the white and blue yarn and weave in ends now or later.

HAND

Rnd 9: Attach the brown yarn in the back loop of the first stitch of rnd 8 (leave a long brown piece of yarn, to use later). In back loops only, sc1 in each stitch around. (18)

Rnds 10–13: Sc1 in each stitch around. (18)

Rnd 14: *Sc1, sc2tog*, repeat around. (12)

Rnd 15: *Sc2tog*, repeat around. (6)

Cut a long tail, weave through the 6 remaining stitches, pull tight, and weave in the end. Stuff the hand and with the brown yarn (of rnd 9) sew the arm closed between rnds 8 and 9. Keep the blue yarn to attach the arm to the body later.

Optional: Continue with flouncing edge as instructed for leg.

HAT

Rnd 1: With blue, start with a magic loop, ch2 (doesn't count as first stitch now and throughout), 6dc in the loop, sl st in first dc. (6)

Rnd 2: With white, ch2, *dc2, 2dc in next*, repeat around, sl st in first dc. (8)

Rnd 3: With blue, ch2, *dc3, 2dc in next*, repeat around, sl st in first dc. (10)

Rnd 4: With white, ch2, *dc4, 2dc in next*, repeat around, sl st in first dc. (12)

Rnd 5: With blue, ch2, *dc5, 2dc in next*, repeat around, sl st in first dc. (14)

Rnd 6: With white, ch2, *dc6, 2dc in next*, repeat around, sl st in first dc. (16)

Rnd 7: With blue, ch2, *dc7, 2dc in next*, repeat around, sl st in first dc. (18)

Rnd 8: With white, ch2, *dc8, 2dc in next*, repeat around, sl st in first dc. (20)

Rnd 9: With blue, ch2, *dc9, 2dc in next*, repeat around, sl st in first dc. (22)

Rnd 10: With white, ch2, *dc10, 2dc in next*, repeat around, sl st in firsl dc. (24)

Rnd 11: With blue, ch2, *dc11, 2dc in next*, repeat around, sl st in first dc. (26)

Rnd 12: With white, ch2, *dc12, 2dc in next*, repeat around, sl st in first dc. (28)

Rnd 13: With blue, ch2, *dc13, 2dc in next*, repeat around, sl st in first dc. (30)

Rnd 14: With white, ch2, *dc9, 2dc in next*, repeat around, sl st in first dc. (33)

Rnd 15: With blue, ch2, *dc10, 2dc in next*, repeat around, sl st in first dc. (36)

Rnd 16: With white, ch2, *dc11, 2dc in next*, repeat around, sl st in first dc. (39)

Rnd 17: With blue, ch2, *dc12, 2dc in next*, repeat around, sl st in first dc. (42)

Rnd 18: With white, ch2, *dc13, 2dc in next*, repeat around, sl st in first dc. (45)

Rnd 19: With blue, ch2, *dc14, 2dc in next*, repeat around, sl st in first dc. (48)

Note: The sizing of the hat also depends on your gauge. You can try the hat on and once you've reached a good fit, you can complete the final rounds without increasing stitches: ch2, dc1 in each stitch around and sl st in first dc.

Rnd 20: With white (you can cut the blue yarn), ch2, *dc15, 2dc in next*, repeat around, sl st in first dc. (51)

Rnd 21: Ch2, *dc16, 2dc in next*, repeat around, sl st in first dc. (54)

Cut a long tail to attach the hat to the head later.

POM-POM FOR HAT

Rnd 1: With white, start with a magic loop, 6sc in the loop. (6)

Rnd 2: 2sc in each stitch around. (12)

Rnd 3: *Sc1, 2sc in next*, repeat around. (18)

Rnd 4: *Sc2, 2sc in next*, repeat around. (24)

Rnd 5: Sc1 in each stitch around. (24)

Rnd 6: *Sc2, sc2tog*, repeat around. (18)

Rnd 7: *Sc1, sc2tog*, repeat around. (12)

Stuff the pom-pom.

Rnd 8: *Sc2tog*, repeat around. (6)

Cut a long tail and attach the pom-pom to the top of the hat.

TAIL

Repeat pom-pom instructions with brown yarn.

This pattern offers a lot of fun possibilities for variations. For example, you can make a rainbow bear or a Christmas bear. But, of course, you can also use the body with pajamas with the head of another ragdoll on it.

PUTTING IT ALL TOGETHER

- Stuff the nose lightly.
- Pin the nose in place on the head between rnds 13 and 19 and sew in place.
- Fold the bottom rnd of the hat double and place on the head.
- Pin both the hat and the ears in place on the hat. Sew the ears to the hat.
- Fold the brim back down again and sew rnd 20 of the hat all the way around to the head. Fold the brim back in place.
- Sew an arm to each side of the body between rnds 1 and 3.
- Sew the tail on the back in the center of the body in rnds 12–14.
- Sew the head to rnd 1 of the body.
- Finally, sew the eyes on the head on each side of the nose in rnds 12–14.

BABY SLEEPY BEAR

DIFFICULTY LEVEL: 3 of 5

SIZE: 6 in (15 cm) tall, excluding cap

MATERIALS

Yarn: DK #3 light weight yarn; shown in Scheepjes Stone Washed
- Brown (Brown Agate 822): 54.5 yd (50 m)
- Gray (Smokey Quartz 842): 65.5 yd (60 m)
- White (Moon Stone 801): 65.5 yd (60 m)
- Black (Black Onyx 803): 22 yd (20 m)

Crochet hook: US size D-3 (3 mm)

Other:
- Fiberfill stuffing
- Needle and scissors

HEAD

Rnd 1: With brown, start with a magic loop, 6sc in the loop. (6)
Rnd 2: 2sc in each stitch around. (12)
Rnd 3: *Sc1, 2sc in next stitch*, repeat around. (18)
Rnd 4: *Sc2, 2sc in next stitch*, repeat around. (24)
Rnd 5: *Sc3, 2sc in next stitch*, repeat around. (30)
Rnds 6–11: Sc1 in each stitch around. (30)
Rnd 12: *Sc3, sc2tog*, repeat around. (24)
Rnd 13: *Sc2, sc2tog*, repeat around. (18)

Stuff the head neatly.

Rnd 14: *Sc1, sc2tog*, repeat around. (12)
Rnd 15: *Sc2tog*, repeat around. (6)

Cut a long tail, weave through the 6 remaining stitches, pull tight, and weave in ends.

NOSE

Rnd 1: With black, start with a magic loop, 6sc in the loop. (6)
Rnd 2: With brown (you can cut the black yarn), 2sc in each stitch around. (12)
Rnd 3: *Sc2, 2sc in next*, repeat around. (16)
Rnd 4: Sc1 in each stitch around. (16)

Cut a long tail to attach the nose to the head later.

EARS (MAKE 2)

Rnd 1: With brown, start with a magic loop, 6sc in the loop. (6)
Rnd 2: 2sc in each stitch around. (12)
Rnd 3: Sc1 in each stitch around. (12)

Cut a long tail to attach the ears to the head later.

BODY

When making the body, hat, and arms, you'll change colors a lot. You can leave the yarn you're not working with and just pick it up whenever you need it. Make sure to not pull the yarn too tight, to keep the fabric nice and relaxed.

Rnd 1: With white (leave a long piece of yarn to use later), ch13, dc1 in 3rd ch from hook, dc9, 3dc in last, continue along the other side of the chains, dc10, 3dc in last, sl st in first dc. (26)
Rnd 2: With gray, ch2 (doesn't count as first stitch now and throughout), *dc12, 2dc in next*, repeat one more time, sl st in first dc. (28)
Rnd 3: With white, ch2, *dc13, 2dc in next*, repeat one more time, sl st in first dc. (30)
Rnd 4: With gray, ch2, *dc14, 2dc in next*, repeat one more time, sl st in first dc. (32)
Rnd 5: With white, ch2, *dc15, 2dc in next*, repeat one more time, sl st in first dc. (34)
Rnd 6: With gray, ch2, *dc16, 2dc in next*, repeat one more time, sl st in first dc. (36)
Rnd 7: With white, ch2, *dc17, 2dc in next*, repeat one more time, sl st in first dc. (38)
Rnd 8: With gray, ch2, *dc18, 2dc in next*, repeat one more time, sl st in first dc. (40)
Rnd 9: With white, ch2, *dc19, 2dc in next*, repeat one more time, sl st in first dc. (42)
Rnd 10: With gray, ch2, *dc20, 2dc in next*, repeat one more time, sl st in first dc. (44)
Rnd 11: With white, ch2, *dc21, 2dc in next*, repeat one more time, sl st in first dc. (46)

Rnd 12: With gray (you can cut the white yarn), ch2, *dc22, ch14, dc1 in 3rd ch from hook, dc1 in each of the remaining 11 chains, 2dc in next dc of rnd 11*, repeat one more time, sl st in first dc.

Cut a long tail to close the body later.

ARMS (MAKE 2)

Rnd 1: With brown, start with a magic loop, 6sc in the loop. (6)
Rnd 2: 2sc in each stitch around. (12)
Rnd 3: *Sc1, 2sc in next*, repeat around. (18)
Rnds 4–5: Sc1 in each stitch around. (18)
Rnd 6: *Sc1, sc2tog*, repeat around. (12)
Rnd 7: Sc1 in each stitch around. (12)
Rnd 8: With white (leave a long brown piece of yarn to use later), sl st 1, ch2 (doesn't count as first stitch now and throughout), dc1 in each stitch around, sl st in first dc. (12)
Rnd 9: With gray, ch2, dc2tog, dc1 in each stitch around, sl st in first dc. (11)
Rnd 10: With white, ch2, dc1 in each stitch around, sl st in first dc. (11)
Rnd 11: With gray, ch2, dc2tog, dc1 in each stitch around, sl st in first dc. (10)
Rnd 12: With white (you can cut the gray yarn), ch2, dc1 in each stitch around, sl st in first dc. (10)

Cut a long tail to attach arms later. Stuff the hand and sew closed between rnds 7 and 8 with the brown yarn.

HAT

Rnd 1: With gray, start with a magic loop, ch2 (doesn't count as first stitch now and throughout), 6dc in the loop, sl st in first dc. (6)
Rnd 2: With white, ch2, dc1 in each stitch around, sl st in first dc. (6)
Rnd 3: With gray, ch2, *dc1, 2dc in next*, repeat around, sl st in first dc. (9)

Rnd 4: With white, ch2, dc1 in each stitch around, sl st in first dc. (9)

Rnd 5: With gray, ch2, *dc2, 2dc in next*, repeat around, sl st in first dc. (12)

Rnd 6: With white, ch2, dc1 in each stitch around, sl st in first dc. (12)

Rnd 7: With gray, ch2, *dc3, 2dc in next*, repeat around, sl st in first dc. (15)

Rnd 8: With white, ch2, dc1 in each stitch around, sl st in first dc. (15)

Rnd 9: With gray, ch2, *dc4, 2dc in next*, repeat around, sl st in first dc. (18)

Rnd 10: With white, ch2, dc1 in each stitch around, sl st in first dc. (18)

Rnd 11: With gray, ch2, *dc2, 2dc in next*, repeat around, sl st in first dc. (24)

Note: The sizing of the hat also depends on your gauge. You can try the hat on and once you've reached a good fit, you can complete the final rounds without increasing stitches: ch2, dc1 in each stitch around and sl st in first dc.

Rnd 12: With white (you can cut the gray yarn), ch2, *dc3, 2dc in next*, repeat around, sl st in first dc. (30)

Rnd 13: Ch2, dc1 in each stitch around, sl st in first dc. (30)

Cut a long tail to attach the hat to the head later.

POM-POM FOR HAT

Rnd 1: With white, start with a magic loop, 6sc in the loop. (6)

Rnd 2: 2sc in each stitch around. (12)

Rnd 3: *Sc1, 2sc in next*, repeat around. (18)

Rnd 4: Sc1 in each stitch around. (18)

Rnd 5: *Sc1, sc2tog*, repeat around. (12)

Stuff the pom-pom.

Rnd 6: *Sc2tog*, repeat around. (6)

Cut a long tail and attach the pom-pom to the top of the hat.

Note: Before assembling, take a look at the photos for assembling the sleeping bear on page 60.

PUTTING IT ALL TOGETHER

- Stuff the nose lightly.
- Pin the nose in place on the head between rnds 7 and 12 and sew in place.
- Fold the bottom rnd of the hat double and pin to the head.
- Fold the brim back down again and sew rnd 12 of the hat all the way around to the head. Fold the brim back in place.
- Pin and sew the ears also to the hat in rnd 12.
- Fold the body in line with the increases to make the belly straight and sew closed with the remaining yarn. Tie a knot in the corners to form the feet.
- Sew an arm to each side of the body between rnds 1 and 2.
- Sew the head to rnd 1 of the body.
- Finally, embroider the eyes on the head on each side of the nose in rnd 7.

DINOSAUR

DIFFICULTY LEVEL: 2 of 5

SIZE: 11.5 in (29 cm) tall

MATERIALS

Yarn: DK #3 light weight yarn; shown in Scheepjes Stone Washed
- Blue (Turquoise 824): 164 yd (150 m)
- Green (New Jade 819): 98.5 yd (90 m)

Crochet hook: US size D-3 (3 mm)

Other:
- Black and gold safety eyes, 15 mm
- Fiberfill stuffing
- Needle and scissors

SPECIAL STITCH

Dc3tog-bobble (dc3tog-b) = Work 3 dc into one stitch (as if working a dc3tog, omitting the final yarn over and pull through of each stitch), finally pulling the last yarn over through all 4 loops on hook to create a bobble.

HEAD

Rnd 1: With blue, start with a magic loop, 6sc in the loop. (6)
Rnd 2: 2sc in each stitch around. (12)
Rnd 3: *Sc1, 2sc in next*, repeat around. (18)
Rnd 4: *Sc2, 2sc in next*, repeat around. (24)
Rnd 5: *Sc3, 2sc in next*, repeat around. (30)
Rnd 6: *Sc4, 2sc in next*, repeat around. (36)
Rnd 7: Sc3, dc3tog in 1 stitch, sc9, dc3tog-b, sc22. (36)

Note: The dc3tog-b makes a tiny bobble to create the nostrils.

Rnds 8–13: Sc1 in each stitch around. (36)
Rnd 14: *Sc5, 2sc in next*, repeat around. (42)
Rnd 15: *Sc6, 2sc in next*, repeat around. (48)
Rnds 16–23: Sc1 in each stitch around. (48)
Rnd 24: *Sc6, sc2tog*, repeat around. (42)
Rnd 25: Sc1 in each stitch around. (42)

Attach the safety eyes between rnds 13 and 14 of the head, 11 stitches apart.

Rnd 26: *Sc5, sc2tog*, repeat around. (36)
Rnd 27: Sc1 in each stitch around. (36)
Rnd 28: *Sc4, sc2tog*, repeat around. (30)
Rnd 29: Sc1 in each stitch around. (30)
Rnd 30: *Sc3, sc2tog*, repeat around. (24)
Rnd 31: *Sc2, sc2tog*, repeat around. (18)

Stuff the head.

Rnd 32: *Sc1, sc2tog*, repeat around. (12)

Cut a long tail, weave through the remaining stitches, and pull tight. Close the seam of the head, and weave in ends.

BODY

You change color often for the body. I like to carry the color I'm not using, rather than cutting it. This means that you put the yarn of the color that you are not using on the stitches to be crocheted and then work around it.

Rnd 1: With blue, ch18, 1dc in 3rd ch from hook, dc14, 3dc in last, continue along the other side of the chains, dc15, 3dc in last, sl st in first dc. (36)

Rnd 2: Ch2 (doesn't count as first stitch now and throughout, so the first dc is made in the same stitch as the ch2), dc3, with green and in back loops only: dc11, with blue: dc3, 2dc in next, dc17, 2dc in last, sl st in first dc. (38)

Rnd 3: With blue: ch2, dc3, with green and in back loops only: dc12, with blue: dc3, 2dc in next, dc18, 2dc in last, sl st in first dc. (40)

Rnd 4: With blue: ch2, dc3, with green and in back loops only: dc13, with blue: dc3, 2dc in next, dc19, 2dc in last, sl st in first dc. (42)

Rnd 5: With blue: ch2, dc3, with green and in back loops only: dc14, with blue: dc3, 2dc in next, dc20, 2dc in last, sl st in first dc. (44)

Rnd 6: With blue: ch2, dc3, with green and in back loops only: dc15, with blue: dc3, 2dc in next, dc21, 2dc in last, sl st in first dc. (46)

Rnd 7: With blue: ch2, dc3, with green and in back loops only: dc16, with blue: dc3, 2dc in next, dc22, 2dc in last, sl st in first dc. (48)

Rnd 8: With blue: ch2, dc3, with green and in back loops only: dc17, with blue: dc3, 2dc in next, dc23, 2dc in last, sl st in first dc. (50)

Rnd 9: With blue: ch2, dc3, with green and in back loops only: dc18, with blue: dc3, 2dc in next, dc24, 2dc in last, sl st in first dc. (52)

Rnd 10: With blue: ch2, dc3, with green and in back loops only: dc19, with blue: dc3, 2dc in next, dc25, 2dc in last, sl st in first dc. (54)

Rnd 11: With blue: ch2, dc3, with green and in back loops only: dc20, with blue: dc3, 2dc in next, dc26, 2dc in last, sl st in first dc. (56)

Rnd 12: With blue: ch2, dc3, with green and in back loops only: dc21, with blue: dc3, 2dc in next, dc27, 2dc in last, sl st in first dc. (58)

Rnd 13: With blue: ch2, dc3, with green and in back loops only: dc22, with blue: dc3, 2dc in next, dc28, 2dc in last, sl st in first dc. (60)

Rnd 14: With blue: ch2, dc3, with green and in back loops only: dc23, with blue: dc3, 2dc in next, dc29, 2dc in last, sl st in first dc. (62)

Rnd 15: With blue: ch2, dc3, with green and in back loops only: dc24, with blue: dc3, 2dc in next, dc30, 2dc in last, sl st in first dc. (64)

Rnd 16: With blue: ch2, dc3, with green and in back loops only: dc25, with blue: dc3, 2dc in next, dc31, 2dc in last, sl st in first dc. (66)

Rnd 17: With blue: ch2, dc3, with green and in back loops only: dc26, with blue: dc3, 2dc in next, dc32, 2dc in last, sl st in first dc. (68)

Rnd 18: With blue: ch2, dc3, with green and in back loops only: dc27, with blue: dc3, 2dc in next, dc33, 2dc in last, sl st in first dc. (70)

Rnd 19: You can cut and weave in the green yarn. With blue: ch2, dc34, 2dc in next, dc34, 2dc in last, sl st in first dc. (72)

Cut a long tail to close the body later. Fold the body in line with the increases to make the belly straight.

ARMS (MAKE 2)

Rnd 1: With green: start with a magic loop, 6sc in the loop. (6)

Rnd 2: 2sc in each stitch around. (12)

Rnd 3: *Sc1, 2sc in next*, repeat around. (18)

Rnd 4: *Sc2, 2sc in next*, repeat around. (24)

Rnd 5: Working in the back loops only: *with blue: sc2, with green: dc3tog-b, repeat from * to * 2 more times, cut the green yarn and weave it in, with blue: sc15. (24)

Rnds 6–8: Sc1 in each stitch around. (24)

Rnd 9: *Sc2, sc2tog*, repeat around. (18)

Rnds 10–11: Sc1 in each stitch around. (18)

Rnd 12: Sl st 1, ch2 (doesn't count as first dc for entire part), dc2tog, dc1 in each stitch around, sl st in first dc. (17)

Rnd 13: Ch2, dc1 in each stitch around, sl st in first dc. (17)

Rnd 14: Ch2, dc2tog, dc1 in each stitch around, sl st in first dc. (16)

Rnd 15: Ch2, dc1 in each stitch around, sl st in first dc. (16)

Rnd 16: Ch2, dc2tog, dc1 in each stitch around, sl st in first dc. (15)

Rnd 17: Ch2, dc1 in each stitch around, sl st in first dc. (15)

Rnd 18: Ch2, dc2tog, dc1 in each stitch around, sl st in first dc. (14)

Cut a long tail to attach arms to body later.

LEGS (MAKE 2)

Repeat instructions for arms from rnd 1 up to and including rnd 15.

Cut yarn and weave in ends.

TAIL

Rnd 1: With blue: start with a magic loop, ch2 (doesn't count as first dc for entire tail), 6dc in the loop, sl st in first dc. (6)

Rnd 2: Ch2, dc1 in each stitch around, sl st in first dc. (6)

Rnd 3: Ch2, *dc1, 2dc in next*, repeat around, sl st in first dc. (9)

Rnd 4: Ch2, dc1 in each stitch around, sl st in first dc. (9)

Rnd 5: Ch2, *dc2, 2dc in next*, repeat around, sl st in first dc. (12)

Rnd 6: Ch2, dc1 in each stitch around, sl st in first dc. (12)

Rnd 7: Ch2, *dc3, 2dc in next*, repeat around, sl st in first dc. (15)

Rnd 8: Ch2, *dc4, 2dc in next*, repeat around, sl st in first dc. (18)

Rnd 9: Ch2, *dc5, 2dc in next*, repeat around, sl st in first dc. (21)

Rnd 10: Ch2, *dc6, 2dc in next*, repeat around, sl st in first dc. (24)

Rnd 11: Ch2, *dc7, 2dc in next*, repeat around, sl st in first dc. (27)

Rnd 12: Ch2, *dc8, 2dc in next*, repeat around, sl st in first dc. (30)

Cut yarn and leave a long tail to sew to body later.

SPIKES (MAKE 7)

Rnd 1: With green, start with a magic loop, ch2 (doesn't count as first dc for entire spike), 6dc in the loop, sl st in first dc. (6)

Rnd 2: Ch2, 2dc in each stitch around, sl st in first dc. (12)

Cut a long tail, sew 2 spikes to head, centering them between the eyes from rnd 23 to rnd 32. The other 5 spikes will go on top of the tail; fold the tail flat and sew them from the base to the tip in one line, as shown in the picture.

PUTTING IT ALL TOGETHER

- Stuff the arms and legs very lightly, just enough to keep them from falling flat. If you're worried the stuffing will come through the double crocheted pieces, you can put the stuffing in a piece of tights or netting.
- Take the body and place both legs between the bottom two layers. With the remaining yarn from the body, sew across the seam with the legs in between. This way you close the bottom and assemble pieces at the same time.
- Sew the tail in the center of the back of the body between rnds 13 and 19.
- Sew an arm to each side of the body between rnds 1 and 3.
- Sew rnd 13 of the head to rnd 1 of the body.

BABY DINOSAUR

DIFFICULTY LEVEL: 2 of 5

SIZE: 6 in (15 cm) tall

MATERIALS

Yarn: DK #3 light weight yarn; shown in Scheepjes Stone Washed
- Blue (Amazonite 813): 109.5 yd (100 m)
- Green (New Jade 819): 54.5 yd (50 m)

Crochet hook: US size D-3 (3 mm)

Other:
- Black and gold safety eyes, 12 mm
- Fiberfill stuffing
- Needle and scissors

SPECIAL STITCH

Dc3tog-bobble (dc3tog-b) = Work 3 dc into 1 stitch (as if working a dc3tog, omitting the final yarn over and pull through of each stitch), finally pulling the last yarn over through all 4 loops on hook to create a bobble.

HEAD

Rnd 1: With blue, start with a magic loop, 6sc in the loop. (6)

Rnd 2: 2sc in each stitch around. (12)

Rnd 3: *Sc1, 2sc in next*, repeat around. (18)

Rnd 4: *Sc2, 2sc in next*, repeat around. (24)

Rnd 5: Sc3, dc3tog-b (to make a bobble for the nostrils), sc7, dc3tog-b, sc12. (24).

Note: The dc3tog-b tends to fall to the inside, so make sure to pop them to the outside.

Rnds 6–8: Sc1 in each stitch around. (24)

Rnd 9: *Sc3, 2sc in next*, repeat around. (30)

Rnd 10: *Sc4, 2sc in next*, repeat around. (36)

Rnds 11–14: Sc1 in each stitch around. (36)

Rnd 15: *Sc4, sc2tog*, repeat around. (30)

Rnd 16: *Sc3, sc2tog*, repeat around. (24)

Rnd 17: *Sc2, sc2tog*, repeat around. (18)

Attach safety eyes between rnds 9 and 10, 7 stitches apart, and stuff the head.

Rnd 18: *Sc1, sc2tog*, repeat around. (12)

Rnd 19: *Sc2tog*, repeat around. (6)

Cut a long piece of yarn, weave through the 6 remaining stitches, pull tight, and leave the end to sew the head to the body later.

BODY

For the body you'll change colors a lot. I like to carry the colors along while using another color. This means that you hold the color you're not using on top of the stitches you are going to work and work around over it, so you won't have loose pieces of yarn on the inside.

Rnd 1: With blue, ch13, dc1 in 3rd ch from hook, dc9, 3dc in last, continue along the other side of the chains, dc10, 3dc in last, sl st in first dc. (26)

Rnd 2: Ch2 (doesn't count as first stitch now and throughout), dc2, with green and in back loops only: dc8, with blue: dc2, 2dc in next, dc12, 2dc in last, sl st in first dc. (28)

Rnd 3: With blue: ch2, dc2, with green and in back loops only: dc9, with blue: dc2, 2dc in next, dc13, 2dc in last, sl st in first dc. (30)

Rnd 4: With blue: ch2, dc2, with green and in back loops only: dc10, with blue: dc2, 2dc in next, dc14, 2dc in last, sl st in first dc. (32)

Rnd 5: With blue: ch2, dc2, with green and in back loops only: dc11, with blue: dc2, 2dc in next, dc15, 2dc in last, sl st in first dc. (34)

Rnd 6: With blue: ch2, dc2, with green and in back loops only: dc12, with blue: dc2, 2dc in next, dc16, 2dc in last, sl st in first dc. (36)

Rnd 7: With blue: ch2, dc2, with green and in back loops only: dc13, with blue: dc2, 2dc in next, dc17, 2dc in last, sl st in first dc. (38)

Rnd 8: With blue: ch2, dc2, with green and in back loops only: dc14, with blue: dc2, 2dc in next, dc18, 2dc in last, sl st in first dc. (40)

Rnd 9: With blue: ch2, dc2, with green and in back loops only: dc15, with blue: dc2, 2dc in next, dc19, 2dc in last, sl st in first dc. (42)

Rnd 10: With blue: ch2, dc2, with green and in back loops only: dc16, with blue: dc2, 2dc in next, dc20, 2dc in last, sl st in first dc. (44)

Rnd 11: With blue: ch2, dc2, with green and in back loops only: dc17, with blue, you can cut the green yarn: dc2, 2dc in next, dc21, 2dc in last, sl st in first dc. (46)

Rnd 12: Ch2, *dc22, ch14, dc1 in 3rd ch from hook, dc1 in each of the remaining 11 chains, 2dc in next dc of rnd 11*, repeat one more time, sl st in first dc.

Cut a long tail to close the body later.

ARMS (MAKE 2)

Rnd 1: With green, start with a magic loop, 6sc in the loop. (6)

Rnd 2: 2sc in each stitch around. (12)

Rnd 3: *Sc1, 2sc in next*, repeat around. (18)

Rnd 4: In back loops only, *with blue, sc1, with green: dc3tog-b, repeat from * to * 2 more times, continue with blue (you can cut the green yarn), sc12. (18)

Rnds 5–6: Sc1 in each stitch around. (18)

Rnd 7: *Sc1, sc2tog*, repeat around. (12)

Rnd 8: Sc1 in each stitch around. (12)

Rnd 9: Sl st 1, ch2 (doesn't count as first stitch now and throughout), dc1 in each stitch around, sl st in first dc. (12)

Rnd 10: Ch2, dc2tog, dc1 in each stitch around, sl st in first dc. (11)

Rnd 11: Ch2, dc1 in each stitch around, sl st in first dc. (11)

Rnd 12: Ch2, dc2tog, dc1 in each stitch around, sl st in first dc. (10)

Stuff the arm very lightly and cut a long tail to attach arms later.

TAIL

Rnd 1: With blue: start with a magic loop, ch2 (doesn't count as first stitch now and throughout), 6dc in the loop, sl st in first dc. (6)

Rnd 2: Ch2, dc1 in each stitch around, sl st in first dc. (6)

Rnd 3: Ch2, *dc1, 2dc in next*, repeat around, sl st in first dc. (9)

Rnd 4: Ch2, *dc2, 2dc in next*, repeat around, sl st in first dc. (12)

Rnd 5: Ch2, *dc3, 2dc in next*, repeat around, sl st in first dc. (15)

Rnd 6: Ch2, *dc4, 2dc in next*, repeat around, sl st in first dc. (18)

Rnd 7: Ch2, *dc5, 2dc in next*, repeat around, sl st in first dc. (21)

Cut a long tail to attach tail later.

SPIKES (MAKE 6)

Rnd 1: With green: start with a magic loop, 6sc in the loop. (6)

Rnd 2: *Sc1, 2sc in next*, repeat around. (9)

Cut a long piece of yarn, sew 2 spikes (folded flat) to the center of the head, from rnds 14 to 19. The other 4 spikes will go on top of the tail; fold the tail flat and sew them from the base to the tip in one line, as shown in the picture on page 69.

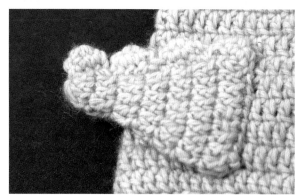

PUTTING IT ALL TOGETHER

- Fold the body in line with the increases to make the belly straight and sew closed with the remaining yarn. Tie a knot in the corners to form the feet.
- Sew an arm to each side of the body between rnds 1 and 2.
- Sew the tail on the back in the center of the body from rnds 8–11.
- Finally, sew the bottom of rnd 7 of the head to rnd 1 of the body.

DRAGON

DIFFICULTY LEVEL: 3 of 5

SIZE: 11.5 in (29 cm) tall

MATERIALS

Yarn: DK #3 light weight yarn; shown in Scheepjes Stone Washed
- Dark blue (Blue Apatite 805): 186 yd (170 m)
- Light blue (Amazonite 813): 120.5 yd (110 m)

Crochet hook: US size D-3 (3 mm)

Other:
- Black and blue safety eyes, 15 mm
- Fiberfill stuffing
- Needle and scissors

The dragon is a variation of the dinosaur ragdoll. First, follow the instructions for the dragon, as on pages 66 to 69, replacing the blue color with dark blue and the green with light blue. Then add the ears and wings, as follows.

EARS (MAKE 2)

Rnd 1: With light blue, start with a magic loop, ch2, 6dc in the loop, sl st in first dc. (6)
Rnd 2: With dark blue (you can cut the light blue yarn), 2dc in each stitch around, sl st in first dc. (12)

Cut a long tail, and sew the ears between rnds 19 and 21 on both sides of the head.

WINGS (MAKE 2)

Row 1: With dark blue, leave a long piece of yarn before the chains to sew on wings later, ch15, sc1 in 2nd ch from hook, sc13. (14)

Row 2: With light blue, turn, ch1 (doesn't count as first stitch now and throughout), sc3, hdc3, dc8, in same stitch as last dc: dc5tog. (15)

Row 3: Turn, ch1, skip the dc5tog, sc14. (14)

Rows 4–5: With dark blue, turn, ch1, sc14. (14)

Rows 6–12: Repeat rows 2–5, ending with row 4.

Sew the wings on the back of the body as shown in the picture, between rows 1 and 4, and weave in ends.

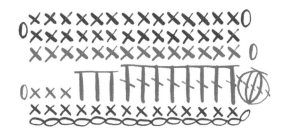

Wing

BABY DRAGON

DIFFICULTY LEVEL: 3 of 5

SIZE: 6 in (15 cm) tall

MATERIALS

Yarn: DK #3 light weight yarn; shown in Scheepjes Stone Washed
- Dark blue (Blue Apatite 805): 131 yd (120 m)
- Lilac (Lilac Quartz 818): 76.5 yd (70 m)

Crochet hook: US size D-3 (3 mm)

Other:
- Black and blue safety eyes, 12 mm
- Fiberfill stuffing
- Needle and scissors

The baby dragon is a variation of the baby dinosaur ragdoll. First, follow the instructions for the baby dragon, as on pages 71 to 73, replacing the blue color with dark blue and the green with lilac. Then add the ears and wings, as follows.

EARS (MAKE 2)

Rnd 1: With lilac, start with a magic loop, 6sc in the loop. (6)
Rnd 2: With dark blue (you can cut the lilac yarn), 2sc in each stitch around. (12)

Cut a long tail and sew the ears between rnds 13 and 14 on both sides of the head.

WINGS (MAKE 2)

Row 1: With dark blue, leave a long piece of yarn before the chains to sew on wings later, ch10, sc1 in 2nd ch from hook, sc8. (9)

Row 2: With lilac, turn, ch1 (doesn't count as first stitch now and throughout), sc2, hdc2, dc5, in same stitch as last dc: dc5tog. (10)

Row 3: Turn, ch1, skip the dc5tog, sc9. (9)

Rows 4–5: With dark blue, turn, ch1, sc9. (9)

Rows 6–12: Repeat rows 2–5, ending with row 4.

Sew the wings on the back of the body as shown in the picture, between rnds 1 and 4, and weave in ends.

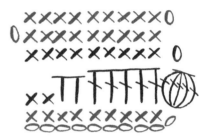

Wing

LION

DIFFICULTY LEVEL: 3 of 5

SIZE: 11.5 in (29 cm)

MATERIALS

Yarn: DK #3 light weight yarn; shown in Scheepjes Stone Washed
- Yellow (Yellow Jasper 809): 164 yd (150 m)
- Brown (Boulder Opal 804): 109.5 yd (100 m)
- Black (Black Onyx 803): 22 yd (20 m)

Crochet hook: US size D-3 (3 mm)

Other:
- Fiberfill stuffing
- Needle and scissors

HEAD

Rnd 1: With yellow, start with a magic loop, 6sc in the loop. (6)

Rnd 2: 2sc in each stitch around. (12)

Rnd 3: *Sc1, 2sc in next stitch*, repeat around. (18)

Rnd 4: *Sc2, 2sc in next stitch*, repeat around. (24)

Rnd 5: *Sc3, 2sc in next stitch*, repeat around. (30)

Rnd 6: *Sc4, 2sc in next stitch*, repeat around. (36)

Rnd 7: *Sc5, 2sc in next stitch*, repeat around. (42)

Rnd 8: *Sc6, 2sc in next stitch*, repeat around. (48)

Rnd 9: *Sc7, 2sc in next stitch*, repeat around. (54)

Rnds 10–13: Sc1 in each stitch around. (54)

Rnd 14: With brown (you can cut the yellow yarn), in back loops only, sc in each stitch around. (54)

Rnd 15: Sc in each stitch around. (54)

Rnd 16: In back loops only, sc in each stitch around. (54)

Rnd 17: Sc in each stitch around. (54)

Rnd 18: In back loops only, *sc7, sc2tog*, repeat around. (48)

Rnd 19: *Sc6, sc2tog*, repeat around. (42)

Rnd 20: In back loops only, *sc5, sc2tog*, repeat around. (36)

Rnd 21: *Sc4, sc2tog*, repeat around. (30)

Rnd 22: In back loops only, *sc3, sc2tog*, repeat around. (24)

Rnd 23: *Sc2, sc2tog*, repeat around. (18)

Stuff the head neatly.

Rnd 24: In back loops only, *sc1, sc2tog*, repeat around. (12)

Rnd 25: *Sc2tog*, repeat around. (6)

Cut a long tail, weave through the 6 remaining stitches, pull tight, and weave in ends.

MANE

Rnd 1: Attach the brown yarn in the first unworked front loop of rnd 13, with the front of the head facing you, *(in 1 stitch: 1sc, ch2, 1dc, 1hdc), skip 1*, repeat from * to * along all of the unworked loops of rnd 13. (27 tufts)

Rnd 2: Now continue in the first unworked front loop of rnd 15, *1sc, skip 2, (in 1 stitch: 4dc, ch3, sl st in first of the 3 chains you just made and 4dc), skip 2*, repeat around. (9 tufts)

Rnd 3: Now continue in the first unworked front loop of rnd 17, (in the first stitch: 1sc, ch2, 1dc, 1hdc, as pictured in chart for rnd 1), skip 1, *sc1, skip 2, (in 1 stitch: 4dc, ch3, sl st in first of the 3 chains you just made and 4dc, as pictured in chart for rnd 2), skip 2*, repeat to last 4 stitches, (in next stitch: sc1, ch2, 1dc, 1hdc, as pictured in chart for rnd 1), skip 3. (10 tufts)

Rnds 4–6: Repeat rnds 2 and 3 into the front loops of rnds 19, 21, and 23, cut the yarn, and weave in ends. Since the number of stitches will decrease, your number of tufts will decrease too. End with 1 sl st in the last loop, cut yarn, and weave in ends.

Mane R1

Mane R2

EARS (MAKE 2)

Rnd 1: With yellow, start with a magic loop, 6sc in the loop. (6)

Rnd 2: *Sc1, 2sc in next stitch*, repeat around. (9)

Rnd 3: Sc1 in each stitch around. (9)

Rnd 4: *Sc2, 2sc in next stitch*, repeat around. (12)

Rnd 5: Sc1 in each stitch around. (12)

Rnd 6: *Sc3, 2sc in next stitch*, repeat around. (15)

Rnds 7–8: Sc1 in each stitch around. (15)

Cut a long tail and sew the ears to the head between rnds 1 and 2 of the mane with 8 stitches in between.

EYES (MAKE 2)

Rnd 1: With black, start with a magic loop, 2sc, 3dc, and 2sc in the loop, pull tight, cut a long tail to attach the eyes slightly above the center of the head in between rnds 5 and 8.

NOSE

Rnd 1: With brown, start with a magic loop, 6sc in the loop. (6)

Rnd 2: Sc1, *3dc in next, sc1*, repeat * to * one more time, 3sc in next stitch, sl st in first sc. (12)

Cut an extra-long tail, sew the nose to the head, centered but slightly lower than the eyes in between rnds 1 and 5. With the remaining yarn embroider a straight line down from the nose for the upper lip and 2 horizontal lines on each side of the face to create lines on the cheeks.

Eyes   Nose

BODY

Rnd 1: With yellow, ch18, 1dc in 3rd ch from hook, dc14, 3dc in last, continue along the other side of the chains, dc15, 3dc in last, sl st in first dc. (36)

Rnd 2: Ch2 (doesn't count as first stitch now and throughout), *dc17, 2dc in next*, repeat one more time, sl st in first dc. (38)

Rnd 3: Ch2, *dc18, 2dc in next*, repeat one more time, sl st in first dc. (40)

Rnd 4: Ch2, *dc19, 2dc in next*, repeat one more time, sl st in first dc. (42)

Rnd 5: Ch2, *dc20, 2dc in next*, repeat one more time, sl st in first dc. (44)

Rnd 6: Ch2, *dc21, 2dc in next*, repeat one more time, sl st in first dc. (46)

Rnd 7: Ch2, *dc22, 2dc in next*, repeat one more time, sl st in first dc. (48)

Rnd 8: Ch2, *dc23, 2dc in next*, repeat one more time, sl st in first dc. (50)

Rnd 9: Ch2, *dc24, 2dc in next*, repeat one more time, sl st in first dc. (52)

Rnd 10: Ch2, *dc25, 2dc in next*, repeat one more time, sl st in first dc. (54)

Rnd 11: Ch2, *dc26, 2dc in next*, repeat one more time, sl st in first dc. (56)

Rnd 12: Ch2, *dc27, 2dc in next*, repeat one more time, sl st in first dc. (58)

Rnd 13: Ch2, *dc28, 2dc in next*, repeat one more time, sl st in first dc. (60)

Rnd 14: Ch2, *dc29, 2dc in next*, repeat one more time, sl st in first dc. (62)

Rnd 15: Ch2, *dc30, 2dc in next*, repeat one more time, sl st in first dc. (64)

Rnd 16: Ch2, *dc31, 2dc in next*, repeat one more time, sl st in first dc. (66)

Rnd 17: Ch2, *dc32, 2dc in next*, repeat one more time, sl st in first dc. (68)

Rnd 18: Ch2, *dc33, 2dc in next*, repeat one more time, sl st in first dc. (70)

Rnd 19: Ch2, *dc34, 2dc in next*, repeat one more time, sl st in first dc. (72)

Cut a long tail to close the body later. Fold the body in line with the increases to make the belly straight.

ARMS (MAKE 2)

Rnd 1: With brown, start with a magic loop, 6sc in the loop. (6)

Rnd 2: 2sc in each stitch around. (12)

Rnd 3: *Sc1, 2sc in next stitch*, repeat around. (18)

Rnd 4: *Sc2, 2sc in next stitch*, repeat around. (24)

Rnds 5–9: Sc1 in each stitch around. (24)

Rnd 10: *Sc2, sc2tog*, repeat around. (18)

Rnds 11–12: Sc1 in each stitch around. (18)

Rnd 13: With yellow (cut an extra-long brown tail to use later), sl st 1, ch2 (doesn't count as first dc now and throughout), dc1 in each stitch around, sl st in first dc. (18)

Rnd 14: Ch2, dc2tog, dc1 in each stitch around, sl st in first dc. (17)

Rnd 15: Ch2, dc1 in each stitch around, sl st in first dc. (17)

At this point, stuff the hand, and take the remaining brown yarn and sew across the arm between rnds 12 and 13.

Rnd 16: Ch2, dc2tog, dc1 in each stitch around, sl st in first dc. (16)

Rnd 17: Ch2, dc1 in each stitch around, sl st in first dc. (16)

Rnd 18: Ch2, dc2tog, dc1 in each stitch around, sl st in first dc. (15)

Cut a long tail to attach arms later.

LEGS (MAKE 2)

Repeat instructions for arm from rnd 1 to rnd 16. Cut yarn and weave in ends.

TAIL

Rnd 1: With brown, start with a magic loop, 6sc in the loop. (6)

Rnd 2: *Sc1, 2sc in next stitch*, repeat around. (9)

Rnd 3: Sc1 in each stitch around. (9)

Rnd 4: *Sc2, 2sc in next stitch*, repeat around. (12)

Rnd 5: Sc1 in each stitch around. (12)

Rnd 6: *Sc3, 2sc in next stitch*, repeat around. (15)

Rnd 7: Sc1 in each stitch around. (15)

Rnd 8: *Sc4, 2sc in next stitch*, repeat around. (18)

Rnd 9: *Sc2, 2sc in next stitch*, repeat around. (24)

Rnd 10: Sc1 in each stitch around. (24)

Rnd 11: *Sc2, sc2tog*, repeat around. (18)

Rnd 12: *Sc4, sc2tog*, repeat around. (15)

Rnd 13: Sc1 in each stitch around. (15)

Rnd 14: With yellow (cut an extra-long brown piece of yarn to use later), sl st 1, ch2 (doesn't count as first dc now and throughout), dc1 in each stitch around, sl st in first dc. (15)

Rnds 15–18: Ch2, dc1 in each stitch around, sl st in first dc. (15)

Stuff the tip of the tail, and take the remaining brown yarn and sew across between rnds 13 and 14. Cut a long tail to attach tail later.

PUTTING IT ALL TOGETHER

- Take the body and place both legs between the bottom two layers. With the remaining yarn from the body, sew across the seam with the legs in between. This way you close the bottom and assemble pieces at the same time.
- Sew the tail on the back in the center of the body in rnds 13–15.
- Sew an arm to each side of the body between rnds 1 and 3.
- Finally, sew rnd 16 of the head to rnd 1 of the body (the mane can playfully pop out on all sides).

BABY LION

DIFFICULTY LEVEL: 3 of 5

SIZE: 5.5 in (14 cm) tall

MATERIALS

Yarn: DK #3 light weight yarn; shown in Scheepjes Stone Washed
- Yellow (Yellow Jasper 809): 142 yd (130 m)
- Brown (Boulder Opal 804): 87.5 yd (80 m)
- Black (Black Onyx 803): 22 yd (20 m)

Crochet hook: US size D-3 (3 mm)

Other:
- Fiberfill stuffing
- Needle and scissors

HEAD

Rnd 1: With yellow, start with a magic loop, 6sc in the loop. (6)

Rnd 2: 2sc in each stitch around. (12)

Rnd 3: *Sc1, 2sc in next stitch*, repeat around. (18)

Rnd 4: *Sc2, 2sc in next stitch*, repeat around. (24)

Rnd 5: *Sc3, 2sc in next stitch*, repeat around. (30)

Rnd 6: *Sc4, 2sc in next stitch*, repeat around. (36)

Rnds 7–8: Sc1 in each stitch around. (36)

Rnd 9: With brown (you can cut the yellow yarn), in back loops only: sc in each stitch around. (36)

Rnd 10: Sc in each stitch around. (36)

Rnd 11: In back loops only, sc in each stitch around. (36)

Rnd 12: *Sc4, sc2tog*, repeat around. (30)

Rnd 13: In back loops only, *sc3, sc2tog*, repeat around. (24)

Rnd 14: *Sc2, sc2tog*, repeat around. (18)

Stuff the head neatly.

Rnd 15: In back loops only, *sc1, sc2tog*, repeat around. (12)

Rnd 16: *Sc2tog*, repeat around. (6)

Cut a long tail, weave through the 6 remaining stitches, pull tight, and weave in ends.

MANE

Rnd 1: Attach the brown yarn in the first un-worked front loop of rnd 8, with the yellow part facing you, *(in 1 stitch: 1sc, ch2, 1dc, 1hdc), skip 1*, repeat from * to * along all of the un-worked loops of rnd 8. (18 tufts)

Rnd 2: Now continue in the first unworked front loop of rnd 10, *1sc, skip 1, (in 1 stitch: 2dc, ch3, sl st in first of the 3 chains you just made and 2dc), skip 1*, repeat from * to * along all of the unworked loops around the entire head until the last 2 loops, skip 1, (in 1 stitch: 2dc, ch3, sl st in first of the 3 chains you just made and 2dc), sl st in same loop as previous dc.

Cut yarn and weave in ends.

Mane R1

Mane R2

EARS (MAKE 2)

Rnd 1: With yellow, start with a magic loop, 6sc in the loop. (6)

Rnd 2: Sc1 in each stitch around. (6)

Rnd 3: *Sc1, 2sc in next stitch*, repeat around. (9)

Rnd 4: *Sc2, 2sc in next stitch*, repeat around. (12)

Rnd 5: Sc1 in each stitch around. (12)

Cut a long tail and sew the ears to the head between rnds 1 and 2 of the mane with 5 stitches in between.

EYES (MAKE 2)

Rnd 1: With black, start with a magic loop, 3sc, 1dc and 3sc in the loop, pull tight, cut a long tail to attach the eyes, slightly above the center of the head between rnds 4 and 6.

Eyes

Nose

NOSE

Rnd 1: With brown, start with a magic loop, 1sc, 2dc, 1sc, 2dc and 2sc in the loop, sl st in first sc. (8)

Cut an extra-long tail, sew the nose to the head, centered but slightly lower than the eyes in between rnds 1 and 2. With the remaining yarn, embroider a straight line down from the nose for the upper lip and 2 horizontal lines on each side of the face to create lines on the cheeks.

BODY

Rnd 1: With yellow, ch13, dc1 in 3rd ch from hook, dc9, 3dc in last, continue along the other side of the chains, dc10, 3dc in last, sl st in first dc. (26)

Rnd 2: Ch2 (doesn't count as first stitch now and throughout), *dc12, 2dc in next*, repeat one more time, sl st in first dc. (28)

Rnd 3: Ch2, *dc13, 2dc in next*, repeat one more time, sl st in first dc. (30)

Rnd 4: Ch2, *dc14, 2dc in next*, repeat one more time, sl st in first dc. (32)

Rnd 5: Ch2, *dc15, 2dc in next*, repeat one more time, sl st in first dc. (34)

Rnd 6: Ch2, *dc16, 2dc in next*, repeat one more time, sl st in first dc. (36)

Rnd 7: Ch2, *dc17, 2dc in next*, repeat one more time, sl st in first dc. (38)

Rnd 8: Ch2, *dc18, 2dc in next*, repeat one more time, sl st in first dc. (40)

Rnd 9: Ch2, *dc19, 2dc in next*, repeat one more time, sl st in first dc. (42)

Rnd 10: Ch2, *dc20, 2dc in next*, repeat one more time, sl st in first dc. (44)

Rnd 11: Ch2, *dc21, 2dc in next*, repeat one more time, sl st in first dc. (46)

Rnd 12: Ch2, *dc22, ch14, dc1 in 3rd ch from hook, dc1 in each of the remaining 11 chains, 2dc in next dc of rnd 11*, repeat one more time, sl st in first dc.

Cut a long tail to close the body later.

ARMS (MAKE 2)

Rnd 1: With brown, start with a magic loop, 6sc in the loop. (6)
Rnd 2: 2sc in each stitch around. (12)
Rnd 3: *Sc1, 2sc in next stitch*, repeat around. (18)
Rnds 4–5: Sc1 in each stitch around. (18)
Rnd 6: *Sc1, sc2tog*, repeat around. (12)
Rnd 7: Sc1 in each stitch around. (12)
Rnd 8: With yellow (cut an extra-long brown tail to use later), sl st 1, ch2 (doesn't count as first dc now and throughout), dc1 in each stitch around, sl st in first dc. (12)
Rnd 9: Ch2, dc2tog, dc1 in each stitch around, sl st in first dc. (11)
Rnd 10: Ch2, dc1 in each stitch around, sl st in first dc. (11)
Rnd 11: Ch2, dc2tog, dc1 in each stitch around, sl st in first dc. (10)
Rnd 12: Ch2, dc1 in each stitch around, sl st in first dc. (10)

At this point, stuff the hand, and take the remaining brown yarn and sew across the arm between rnds 7 and 8.

Cut a long tail to attach arms later.

TAIL

Rnd 1: With brown, start with a magic loop, 6sc in the loop. (6)
Rnd 2: Sc1 in each stitch around. (6)
Rnd 3: *Sc1, 2sc in next stitch*, repeat around. (9)
Rnd 4: *Sc2, 2sc in next stitch*, repeat around. (12)
Rnd 5: Sc1 in each stitch around. (12)
Rnd 6: *Sc1, 2sc in next stitch*, repeat around. (18)
Rnd 7: Sc1 in each stitch around. (18)
Rnd 8: *Sc1, sc2tog*, repeat around. (12)
Rnd 9: *Sc1, sc2tog*, repeat around. (8)
Rnd 10: With yellow (cut an extra-long brown piece of yarn to use later), sl st 1, ch2 (doesn't count as first dc now and throughout), dc1 in each stitch around, sl st in first dc. (8)

Stuff the tip of the tail, and take the remaining brown yarn and sew across between rnds 9 and 10.

Rnds 11–12: Ch2, dc1 in each stitch around, sl st in first dc. (8)

Cut a long tail to attach tail later.

PUTTING IT ALL TOGETHER

- Fold the body in line with the increases to make the belly straight and sew closed with the remaining yarn. Tie a knot in the corners to form the feet.
- Sew the tail on the back in the center of the body in rnds 9 and 10.
- Sew an arm to each side of the body between rnds 1 and 2.
- Finally, sew rnd 11 of the head to rnd 1 of the body (the mane can playfully pop out on all sides).

LEOPARD

DIFFICULTY LEVEL: 4 of 5

SIZE: 12.5 in (32 cm) tall

MATERIALS

Yarn: DK #3 light weight yarn; shown in Scheepjes Stone Washed
- Yellow (Yellow Jasper 809): 131 yd (120 m)
- Brown (Brown Agate 822): 109.5 yd (100 m)
- Black (Black Onyx 803): 109.5 yd (100 m)
- White (Moon Stone 801): 54.5 yd (50 m)

Crochet hook: US size D-3 (3 mm)

Other:
- Mint and black safety eyes, 15 mm
- Fiberfill stuffing
- Needle and scissors

HEAD

Rnd 1: With yellow, start with a magic loop, 6sc in the loop. (6)

Rnd 2: 2sc in each stitch around. (12)

Rnd 3: *Sc1, 2sc in next*, repeat around. (18)

Rnd 4: *Yellow: sc1, black: sc1, yellow: 2sc in next*, repeat around. (24)

Rnd 5: *Yellow: sc3, 2sc in next*, repeat around. (30)

Rnd 6: *Black: sc2, yellow: sc2, 2sc in next*, repeat around. (36)

Rnd 7: *Black: sc1, brown: sc1, yellow: sc2, black: sc1, yellow: 2sc in next*, repeat around. (42)

Rnd 8: *Yellow: sc4, black: sc2, yellow: 2sc in next*, repeat around. (48)

Rnd 9: *Yellow: sc7, 2sc in next*, repeat around. (54)

Rnd 10: *Yellow: sc1, black: sc2, yellow: sc3, black: sc2, yellow: sc1*, repeat around. (54)

Rnd 11: *Yellow: sc1, brown: sc1, black: sc1, yellow: sc3, brown: sc1, black: sc2*, repeat around. (54)

Rnd 12: *Yellow: sc5, black: sc1, brown: sc2, black: sc1*, repeat around. (54)

Rnd 13: *Yellow: sc1, black: sc2, yellow: sc2, black: sc4*, repeat around. (54)

Rnd 14: *Yellow: sc1, brown: sc2, black: sc1, yellow: sc5*, repeat around. (54)

Rnd 15: *Yellow: sc1, black: sc1, brown: sc1, yellow: sc2, black: sc2, yellow: sc2*, repeat around. (54)

Rnd 16: *Yellow: sc5, black: sc1, brown: sc2, black: sc1*, repeat around. (54)

Rnd 17: *Yellow: sc1, black: sc2, yellow: sc3, brown: sc2, black: sc1*, repeat around. (54)

Rnd 18: *Yellow: sc1, black: sc2, yellow: sc3, black: sc3*, repeat around. (54)

Rnd 19: With white (you can cut all other yarns), *sc7, sc2tog*, repeat around. (48)

Rnd 20: *Sc6, sc2tog*, repeat around. (42)

Rnd 21: *Sc5, sc2tog*, repeat around. (36)

Rnd 22: *Sc4, sc2tog*, repeat around. (30)

Rnd 23: *Sc3, sc2tog*, repeat around. (24)

Rnd 24: *Sc2, sc2tog*, repeat around. (18)

Attach the eyes between rnds 14 and 15, 11 stitches apart, and stuff the head.

Rnd 25: *Sc1, sc2tog*, repeat around. (12)

Rnd 26: *Sc2tog*, repeat around. (6)

Cut a long tail, weave through the 6 remaining stitches, pull tight, and weave in ends.

NOSE

Rnd 1: With black, start with a magic loop, 1sc, 2dc, 1sc, 2dc, 1sc, and 2dc. (9)

Rnd 2: With white (you can cut the black yarn), 2sc in first stitch, 3sc in next stitch, sc3, 3sc in next stitch, 2sc in next stitch, sc2. (15)

Rnd 3: Sc3, 2sc in each of the next 2 stitches, sc3, 2sc in each of the next 2 stitches, sc5. (19)

Rnd 4: Sc4, 2sc in each of the next 2 stitches, sc5, 2sc in each of the next 2 stitches, sc6, sl st in first sc. (23)

Cut an extra-long tail and sew the nose to the head over rnds 15–20.

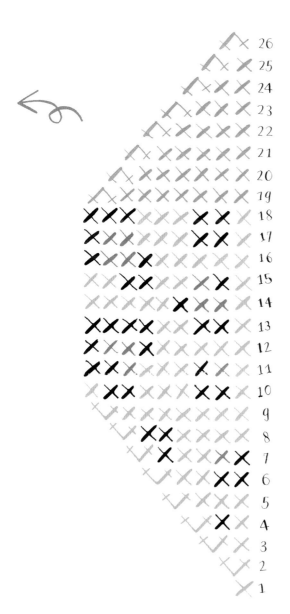

Head

Nose

EARS (MAKE 2)

Rnd 1: With yellow, start with a magic loop, 6sc in the loop. (6)
Rnd 2: *Sc1, 2sc in next stitch*, repeat around. (9)
Rnd 3: Sc1 in each stitch around. (9)
Rnd 4: *Sc2, 2sc in next stitch*, repeat around. (12)
Rnd 5: Sc1 in each stitch around. (12)
Rnd 6: *Sc3, 2sc in next stitch*, repeat around. (15)
Rnds 7 and 8: Sc1 in each stitch around. (15)

Cut a long tail and sew the ears to the head between rnds 4 and 8 on both sides of the head.

BODY

Rnd 1: With yellow, ch18, 1dc in 3rd ch from hook, dc14, 3dc in last, continue along the other side of the chains, dc15, 3dc in last, sl st in first dc. (36)
Rnd 2: Yellow: ch2 (doesn't count as first stitch now and throughout), *yellow: dc2, black: dc1, brown: dc1, black: dc1, yellow: dc4, black: dc1, brown: dc2, black: dc1, yellow: dc4, 2dc in next*, repeat from * to * one more time, sl st in first dc. (38)

Rnd 3: Yellow: ch2, *yellow: dc3, brown: dc2, black: dc1, yellow: dc4, black: dc1, brown: dc1, black: dc1, yellow: dc3, black: dc2, yellow: 2dc in next*, repeat from * to * one more time, sl st in first dc. (40)
Rnd 4: Yellow: ch2, *yellow: dc4, black: dc2, yellow: dc9, black: dc1, brown: dc2, black: dc1, yellow: 2dc in next*, repeat from * to * one more time, sl st in first dc. (42)
Rnd 5: Yellow: ch2, *yellow: dc8, black: dc1, brown: dc2, black: dc2, yellow: dc3, black: dc1, brown: dc1, black: dc1, yellow: dc1, 2dc in next*, repeat from * to * one more time, sl st in first dc. (44)
Rnd 6: Yellow: ch2, *yellow: dc1, black: dc1, brown: dc1, black: dc1, yellow: dc4, black: dc1, brown: dc3, black: dc1, yellow: dc8, 2dc in next*, repeat from * to * one more time, sl st in first dc. (46)
Rnd 7: Yellow: ch2, *yellow: dc1, black: dc1, brown: dc2, yellow: dc4, black: dc2, yellow: dc7, black: dc3, yellow: dc2, 2dc in next*, repeat from * to * one more time, sl st in first dc. (48)
Rnd 8: Yellow: ch2, *yellow: dc5, black: dc2, yellow: dc5, black: dc2, yellow: dc3, black: dc1, brown: dc3, black: dc1, yellow: dc1, 2dc in next*, repeat from * to * one more time, sl st in first dc. (50)
Rnd 9: Yellow: ch2, *yellow: dc3, black: dc2, brown: dc2, black: dc1, yellow: dc4, black: dc3, yellow: dc3, black: dc1, brown: dc2, black: dc2, yellow: dc1, 2dc in next*, repeat from * to * one more time, sl st in first dc. (52)
Rnd 10: Yellow: ch2, *yellow: dc4, black: dc2, brown: dc1, black: dc1, yellow: dc17, 2dc in next*, repeat from * to * one more time, sl st in first dc. (54)
Rnd 11: Yellow: ch2, *yellow: dc10, black: dc2, yellow: dc3, black: dc2, brown: dc1, black: dc1, yellow: dc4, brown: dc1, black: dc1, yellow: dc1, 2dc in next*, repeat from * to * one more time, sl st in first dc. (56)

Rnd 12: Yellow: ch2, *yellow: dc1, black: dc1, brown: dc1, black: dc1, yellow: dc4, black: dc1, brown: dc3, black: dc1, yellow: dc3, black: dc1, brown: dc1, black: dc1, yellow: dc3, black: dc1, brown: dc2, black: dc1, yellow: dc1, 2dc in next*, repeat from * to * one more time, sl st in first dc. (58)

Rnd 13: Yellow: ch2, *yellow: dc1, black: dc3, yellow: dc4, black: dc2, brown: dc2, black: dc1, yellow: dc10, black: dc2, yellow: dc3, 2dc in next*, repeat from * to * one more time, sl st in first dc. (60)

Rnd 14: Yellow: ch2, *yellow: dc5, black: dc2, yellow: dc10, brown: dc1, black: dc2, yellow: dc6, black: dc2, yellow: dc1, 2dc in next*, repeat from * to * one more time, sl st in first dc. (62)

Rnd 15: Yellow: ch2, *yellow: dc2, black: dc2, brown: dc3, black: dc1, yellow: dc2, brown: dc1, black: dc1, yellow: dc4, black: dc1, brown: dc3, black: dc1, yellow: dc5, black: dc1, brown: dc1, black: dc1, yellow: dc1, 2dc in next*, repeat from * to * one more time, sl st in first dc. (64)

Rnd 16: Yellow: ch2, *yellow: dc4, black: dc1, brown: dc2, black: dc1, yellow: dc2, black: dc2, yellow: dc5, black: dc2, brown: dc2, yellow: dc3, black: dc2, yellow: dc5, 2dc in next*, repeat from * to * one more time, sl st in first dc. (66)

Rnd 17: Yellow: ch2, *yellow: dc1, black: dc1, yellow: dc12, black: dc1, brown: dc1, yellow: dc8, black: dc2, brown: dc2, black: dc2, yellow: dc2, 2dc in next*, repeat from * to * one more time, sl st in first dc. (68)

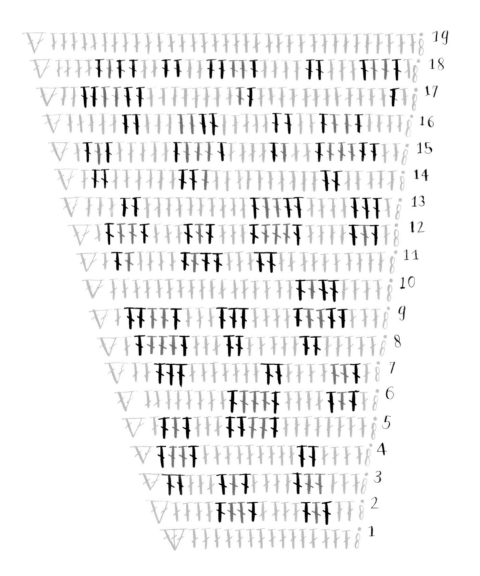

Rnd 18: Yellow: ch2, *yellow: dc1, black: dc1, brown: dc2, black: dc1, yellow: dc3, black: dc2, yellow: dc4, black: dc1, brown: dc2, black: dc2, yellow: dc2, black: dc2, yellow: dc2, black: dc2, brown: dc1, black: dc1, yellow: dc4, 2dc in next*, repeat from * to * one more time, sl st in first dc. (70)

Rnd 19: With yellow (you can cut the brown and black yarn), ch2, *dc34, 2dc in next*, repeat from * to * one more time, sl st in first dc. (72)

Cut a long tail to close the body later. Fold the body in line with the increases to make the belly straight.

ARMS (MAKE 2)

Rnd 1: With white, start with a magic loop, 6sc in the loop. (6)

Rnd 2: 2sc in each stitch around. (12)

Rnd 3: *Sc1, 2sc in next*, repeat around. (18)

Rnd 4: *Sc2, 2sc in next*, repeat around. (24)

Rnds 5–9: Sc1 in each stitch around. (24)

Rnd 10: *Sc2, sc2tog*, repeat around. (18)

Rnds 11–12: Sc1 in each stitch around. (18)

Rnd 13: With yellow (cut an extra-long piece of white yarn to use later), sl st 1, ch2 (doesn't count as first stitch now and throughout), *yellow: dc7, black: dc2*, repeat from * to * one more time, sl st in first dc. (18)

Rnd 14: Yellow: ch2, *yellow: dc2tog, black: dc1, brown: dc2, black: dc1, yellow: dc3*, repeat from * to * one more time, sl st in first dc. (16)

Rnd 15: Yellow: ch2, *yellow: dc2, black: dc1, brown: dc1, black: dc1, yellow: dc3*, repeat from * to * one more time, sl st in first dc. (16)

At this point, stuff the hand, and take the remaining white yarn and sew across the arm between rnds 12 and 13.

Rnd 16: Yellow: ch2, *yellow: dc2tog, dc4, black: dc2*, repeat from * to * one more time, sl st in first dc. (14)

Rnd 17: Yellow: ch2, *yellow: dc3, black: dc1, brown: dc2, black: dc1*, repeat from * to * one more time, sl st in first dc. (14)

Rnd 18: With yellow (cut the brown and black yarn), ch2, dc1 in each stitch around, sl st in first st. (14)

Cut a long tail to attach arms later.

LEGS (MAKE 2)

Repeat instructions for arm from rnd 1 to rnd 16. Cut yarn and weave in ends.

TAIL

Rnd 1: With yellow, start with a magic loop, ch2, 12dc in the loop, sl st in first dc. (12)

Rnds 2–3: Yellow: ch2, *yellow: dc2, black: dc1, brown: dc2, black: dc1*, repeat from * to * one more time, sl st in first dc. (12)

Rnd 4: Yellow: ch2, dc1 in each stitch around, sl st in first dc. (12)

Rnd 5: Yellow: ch2, *yellow: dc1, black: dc1, brown: dc1, black: dc1, yellow: dc2*, repeat from * to * one more time, sl st in first dc. (12)

Rnd 6: Yellow: ch2, *yellow: dc2, brown: dc1, black: dc1, yellow: dc2*, repeat from * to * one more time, sl st in first dc. (12)

Rnd 7: Yellow: ch2, dc1 in each stitch around, sl st in first dc. (12)

Rnd 8: Yellow: ch2, *yellow: dc3, black: dc2, yellow: dc1*, repeat from * to * one more time, sl st in first dc. (12)

Rnd 9: With yellow (cut the brown and black yarn), ch2, dc1 in each stitch around, sl st in first dc. (12)

Cut a long tail to attach the tail later.

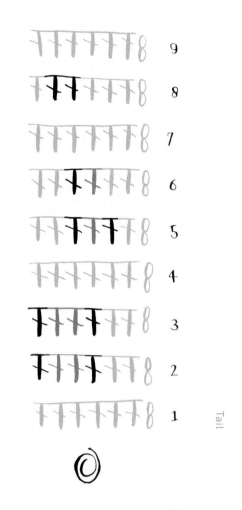

18

17

16

15

14

13

Arms

9

8

7

6

5

4

3

2

1

Tail

PUTTING IT ALL TOGETHER

- Take the body and place both legs between the bottom two layers. With the remaining yarn from the body, sew across the seam with the legs in between. This way you close the bottom and assemble pieces at the same time.
- Sew the tail on the back in the center of the body in rnds 13 and 14.
- Sew an arm to each side of the body between rnds 1 and 3.
- Finally, sew rnd 17 of the head to rnd 1 of the body.

BABY LEOPARD

DIFFICULTY LEVEL: 4 of 5

SIZE: 7.5 in (19 cm) tall

MATERIALS

Yarn: DK #3 light weight yarn; shown in Scheepjes Stone Washed
- Yellow (Yellow Jasper 809): 87.5 yd (80 m)
- Brown (Brown Agate 822): 54.5 yd (50 m)
- Black (Black Onyx 803): 54.5 yd (50 m)
- White (Moon Stone 801): 33 yd (30 m)

Crochet hook: US size D-3 (3 mm)

Other:
- Mint and black safety eyes, 12 mm
- Fiberfill stuffing
- Needle and scissors

HEAD

Rnd 1: With yellow, start with a magic loop, 6sc in the loop. (6)
Rnd 2: 2sc in each stitch around. (12)
Rnd 3: *Sc1, 2sc in next*, repeat around. (18)
Rnd 4: *Yellow: sc1, black: sc1, yellow: 2sc in next*, repeat around. (24)
Rnd 5: *Yellow: sc3, 2sc in next*, repeat around. (30)
Rnd 6: *Black: sc2, yellow: sc2, 2sc in next*, repeat around. (36)
Rnd 7: *Brown: sc2, black: sc1, yellow: sc3*, repeat around. (36)
Rnd 8: *Yellow: sc1, black: sc1, yellow: sc2, black: sc2*, repeat around. (36)
Rnd 9: *Yellow: sc3, black: sc1, brown: sc2*, repeat around. (36)
Rnd 10: *Yellow: sc3, black: sc3*, repeat around. (36)
Rnd 11: *Yellow: sc1, black: sc1, yellow: sc4*, repeat around. (36)
Rnds 12–13: *Yellow: sc1, black: sc1, brown: sc1, black: sc1, yellow: sc2*, repeat around. (36)
Rnd 14: With white (you can cut all other yarns), *sc4, sc2tog*, repeat around. (30)
Rnd 15: *Sc3, sc2tog*, repeat around. (24)
Rnd 16: *Sc2, sc2tog*, repeat around. (18)

Attach the eyes between rnds 11 and 12, 7 stitches apart, and stuff the head.

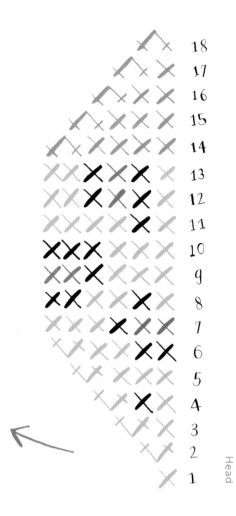

Head

EARS (MAKE 2)

Rnd 1: With yellow, start with a magic loop, 6sc in the loop. (6)
Rnd 2: Sc1 in each stitch around. (6)
Rnd 3: *Sc1, 2sc in next stitch*, repeat around. (9)
Rnd 4: *Sc2, 2sc in next stitch*, repeat around. (12)
Rnd 5: Sc1 in each stitch around. (12)

Cut a long tail and sew the ears to the head between rnds 4 and 7 on both sides of the head.

Rnd 17: *Sc1, sc2tog*, repeat around. (12)
Rnd 18: *Sc2tog*, repeat around. (6)

Cut a long tail, weave through the 6 remaining stitches, pull tight, and weave in ends.

NOSE

Rnd 1: With black, start with a magic loop, *1sc, 1dc, 1sc, 1dc, 1sc, and 1dc in the loop. (6)
Rnd 2: With white (you can cut the black yarn), 2sc in first stitch, 3sc in next stitch, sc1, 3sc in next stitch, 2sc in next stitch, 1sc in last stitch, sl st in first sc. (12)

Cut a long tail and sew the nose to the head over rnds 12–15.

Nose

BODY

Rnd 1: With yellow, ch13, dc1 in 3rd ch from hook, dc9, 3dc in last, continue along the other side of the chains, dc10, 3dc in last, sl st in first dc. (26)

Rnd 2: Yellow: ch2 (doesn't count as first stitch now and throughout), *yellow: dc1, black: dc1, brown: dc1, black: dc1, yellow: dc4, black: dc1, brown: dc2, black: dc1, yellow: 2dc in next*, repeat from * to * one more time, sl st in first dc. (28)

Rnd 3: Yellow: ch2, *yellow: dc2, brown: dc2, black: dc1, yellow: dc4, black: dc1, brown: dc1, black: dc1, yellow: dc1, 2dc in next*, repeat from * to * one more time, sl st in first dc. (30)

Rnd 4: Yellow: ch2, *yellow: dc3, black: dc2, yellow: dc9, 2dc in next*, repeat from * to * one more time, sl st in first dc. (32)

Rnd 5: Yellow: ch2, *yellow: dc7, black: dc1, brown: dc2, black: dc2, yellow: dc3, 2dc in next*, repeat from * to * one more time, sl st in first dc. (34)

Rnd 6: Yellow: ch2, *yellow: dc1, black: dc1, brown: dc1, black: dc1, yellow: dc3, black: dc1, brown: dc3, black: dc1, yellow: dc2, black: dc2, yellow: 2dc in next*, repeat from * to * one more time, sl st in first dc. (36)

Rnd 7: Yellow: ch2, *yellow: dc1, black: dc1, brown: dc2, black: dc1, yellow: dc2, black: dc2, yellow: dc5, black: dc1, brown: dc1, black: dc1, yellow: 2dc in next*, repeat from * to * one more time, sl st in first dc. (38)

Rnd 8: Yellow: ch2, *yellow: dc2, black: dc2, yellow: dc7, black: dc2, yellow: dc2, black: dc1, brown: dc1, black: dc1, yellow: 2dc in next*, repeat from * to * one more time, sl st in first dc. (40)

Rnd 9: Yellow: ch2, *yellow: dc6, black: dc2, yellow: dc3, black: dc3, yellow: dc5, 2dc in next*, repeat from * to * one more time, sl st in first dc. (42)

Rnd 10: Yellow: ch2, *yellow: dc1, black: dc2, yellow: dc2, black: dc1, brown: dc2, black: dc1, yellow: dc6, black: dc2, brown: dc2, black: dc1, yellow: 2dc in next*, repeat from * to * one more time, sl st in first dc. (44)

Rnd 11: Yellow: ch2, *yellow: dc1, black: dc2, yellow: dc2, black: dc1, brown: dc3, black: dc2, yellow: dc5, black: dc1, brown: dc3, black: dc1, yellow: 2dc in next*, repeat from * to * one more time, sl st in first dc. (46)

Rnd 12: With yellow (you can cut the brown and black yarn), ch2, *dc22, ch14, dc1 in 3rd ch from hook, dc1 in each of the remaining 11 chains, 2dc in next dc of rnd 11*, repeat one more time, sl st in first dc.

Cut a long tail to close the body later.

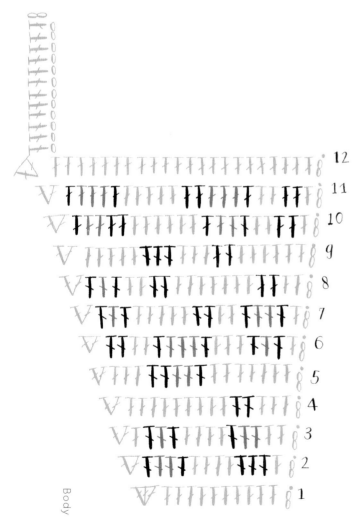

Body

ARMS (MAKE 2)

Rnd 1: With white, start with a magic loop, 6sc in the loop. (6)

Rnd 2: 2sc in each stitch around. (12)

Rnd 3: *Sc1, 2sc in next stitch*, repeat around. (18)

Rnds 4–5: Sc1 in each stitch around. (18)

Rnd 6: *Sc1, sc2tog*, repeat around. (12)

Rnd 7: Sc1 in each stitch around. (12)

Rnd 8: With yellow (cut an extra-long white tail to use later), sl st 1, ch2 (doesn't count as first dc now and throughout), dc1 in each stitch around, sl st in first dc. (12)

Rnd 9: Yellow: ch2, *yellow: dc2tog, black: dc1, brown: dc2, black: dc1*, repeat one more time, sl st in first dc. (10)

Rnd 10: Yellow: ch2, *yellow: dc2, black: dc1, brown: dc1, black: dc1*, repeat one more time. (10)

Rnd 11: Yellow: ch2, *dc2tog, dc1 in each stitch around*, repeat one more time, sl st in first dc. (8)

Rnd 12: Black: ch2, *black: dc2, yellow: dc2*, repeat one more time, sl st in first dc. (8)

At this point, stuff the hand, and take the remaining white yarn and sew across the arm between rnds 7 and 8. Cut a long tail to attach arms later.

TAIL

Rnd 1: With yellow, start with a magic loop, ch2 (doesn't count as first dc now and throughout), 8dc in the loop, sl st in first dc. (8)

Rnds 2–3: Yellow: ch2, *yellow: dc1, brown: dc2, black: dc1*, repeat one more time, sl st in first dc. (8)

Rnd 4: Yellow: ch2, dc1 in each stitch around, sl st in first dc. (8)

Rnd 5: Brown: ch2, *brown: dc1, black: dc1, yellow: dc2*, repeat one more time, sl st in first dc. (8)

Cut a long tail to attach tail later.

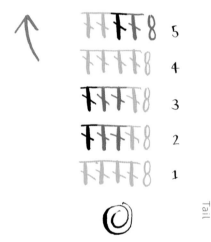

Of course, a cuddly toy does not
always have to be crocheted in true-
to-life shades. For example, what do
you think of these funky leopards?

PUTTING IT ALL TOGETHER

- Fold the body in line with the increases to make the belly straight and sew
  closed with the remaining yarn. Tie a knot in the corners to form the feet.
- Sew the tail on the back in the center of the body in rnds 8 and 9.
- Sew an arm to each side of the body between rnds 1 and 2.
- Finally, sew rnd 14 of the head to rnd 1 of the body.

SLOTH

DIFFICULTY LEVEL: 3 of 5

SIZE: 10 in (25 cm) tall

MATERIALS

Yarn: DK #3 light weight yarn;
shown in Scheepjes Stone
Washed
- White (Moon Stone 801):
  54.5 yd (50 m)
- Beige (Boulder Opal
  804): 197 yd (180 m)
- Brown (Brown Agate
  822): 22 yd (20 m)

Crochet hook: US size D-3
(3 mm)

Other:
- Brown and black safety
  eyes, 15 mm
- Fiberfill stuffing
- Needle and scissors

RIGHT EYE

Rnd 1: With brown, start with a magic loop, 6sc in
the loop. (6) Don't pull loop too tight, so safety
eye can fit through.

Rnd 2: Sl st 1, ch3, 2tr in same as previous sl st,
2dc in next stitch, 2hdc in next stitch, 2sc in
each of the next 3 stitches, sl st in same as last
sc. (12)

Cut a long tail, insert safety eye in center of
magic loop, but don't secure yet! Continue with
left eye.

LEFT EYE

Rnd 1: With brown, start with a magic loop, 6sc in
the loop. (6) Don't pull loop too tight, so safety
eye can fit through.

Rnd 2: 2sc in each of the first 3 stitches, 2hdc in
next, 2dc in next, 2tr in next, ch3, sl st in same
as previous tr. (12)

Cut a long tail, insert safety eye in center of magic loop, but don't secure yet! Continue with nose.

Rnd 4: *Sc2, 2sc in next*, repeat around. (24)
Rnd 5: *Sc3, 2sc in next*, repeat around. (30)
Rnd 6: *Sc4, 2sc in next*, repeat around. (36)
Rnd 7: *Sc5, 2sc in next*, repeat around. (42)
Rnd 8: *Sc6, 2sc in next*, repeat around. (48)
Rnd 9: *Sc7, 2sc in next*, repeat around. (54)
Rnd 10: Change to beige (cut the white yarn), *sc8, 2sc in next*, repeat around. (60)
Rnd 11: *Sc9, 2sc in next*, repeat around. (66)
Rnd 12: *Sc10, 2sc in next*, repeat around. (72)
Rnds 13–17: Sc1 in each stitch around. (72)
Rnd 18: *Sc10, sc2tog*, repeat around. (66)
Rnd 19: *Sc9, sc2tog*, repeat around. (60)
Rnd 20: *Sc8, sc2tog*, repeat around. (54)
Rnd 21: *Sc7, sc2tog*, repeat around. (48)
Rnd 22: *Sc6, sc2tog*, repeat around. (42)
Rnd 23: *Sc5, sc2tog*, repeat around. (36)
Rnd 24: *Sc4, sc2tog*, repeat around. (30)

Place the eyes between rnds 3 and 9 on both sides of the head, in the corner over the color change. Secure safety eye through both layers and sew eye in place with remaining yarn. Take the nose and with the increases on each side place between the eyes and sew in place (the bottom should be a bit lower than the eyes).

Rnd 25: *Sc3, sc2tog*, repeat around. (24)
Rnd 26: *Sc2, sc2tog*, repeat around. (18)

Stuff the head firmly.

Rnd 27: *Sc1, sc2tog*, repeat around. (12)
Rnd 28: *Sc2tog*, repeat around. (6)

Cut a long tail, weave through the 6 remaining stitches, pull tight, and save to attach the head later.

NOSE

Rnd 1: With brown, start with a magic loop, 6sc in the loop. (6)
Rnd 2: 4sc in first stitch, sc3, 4sc in next stitch, sc1, sl st in first sc. (12)

Cut a long tail and continue with head.

HEAD

Rnd 1: With white, start with a magic loop, 6sc in the loop. (6)
Rnd 2: 2sc in each stitch around. (12)
Rnd 3: *Sc1, 2sc in next*, repeat around. (18)

BODY

Rnd 1: With beige, ch18, 1dc in 3rd ch from hook, dc14, 3dc in last, continue along the other side of the chains, dc15, 3dc in last, sl st in first dc. (36)

Rnd 2: Ch2 (doesn't count as first stitch now and throughout), *dc17, 2dc in next*, repeat one more time, sl st in first dc. (38)

Rnd 3: Ch2, *dc18, 2dc in next*, repeat one more time, sl st in first dc. (40)

Rnd 4: Ch2, *dc19, 2dc in next*, repeat one more time, sl st in first dc. (42)

Rnd 5: Ch2, *dc20, 2dc in next*, repeat one more time, sl st in first dc. (44)

Rnd 6: Ch2, *dc21, 2dc in next*, repeat one more time, sl st in first dc. (46)

Rnd 7: Ch2, *dc22, 2dc in next*, repeat one more time, sl st in first dc. (48)

Rnd 8: Ch2, *dc23, 2dc in next*, repeat one more time, sl st in first dc. (50)

Rnd 9: Ch2, *dc24, 2dc in next*, repeat one more time, sl st in first dc. (52)

Rnd 10: Ch2, *dc25, 2dc in next*, repeat one more time, sl st in first dc. (54)

Rnd 11: Ch2, *dc26, 2dc in next*, repeat one more time, sl st in first dc. (56)

Rnd 12: Ch2, *dc27, 2dc in next*, repeat one more time, sl st in first dc. (58)

Rnd 13: Ch2, *dc28, 2dc in next*, repeat one more time, sl st in first dc. (60)

Rnd 14: Ch2, *dc29, 2dc in next*, repeat one more time, sl st in first dc. (62)

Rnd 15: Ch2, *dc30, 2dc in next*, repeat one more time, sl st in first dc. (64)

Rnd 16: Ch2, *dc31, 2dc in next*, repeat one more time, sl st in first dc. (66)

Cut a long tail to close the body later. Fold the body in line with the increases to make the belly straight.

ARMS (MAKE 2)

Rnd 1: With beige: start with a magic loop, 6sc in the loop. (6)

Rnd 2: 2sc in each stitch around. (12)

Rnd 3: *Sc1, 2sc in next*, repeat around. (18)

Rnd 4: *Sc2, 2sc in next*, repeat around. (24)

Rnd 5: *With beige: sc2, with white: dc3tog in 1 stitch*, repeat from * to * 2 more times, cut the white yarn and weave it in, with beige: sc15. (24)

Rnds 6–8: Sc1 in each stitch around. (24)

Rnd 9: *Sc2, sc2tog*, repeat around. (18)

Rnds 10–11: Sc1 in each stitch around. (18)

Rnd 12: Sl st 1, ch2 (doesn't count as first dc for entire part), dc2tog, dc1 in each stitch around, sl st in first dc. (17)

Rnd 13: Ch2, dc1 in each stitch around, sl st in first dc. (17)

Rnd 14: Ch2, dc2tog, dc1 in each stitch around, sl st in first dc. (16)

Rnd 15: Ch2, dc1 in each stitch around, sl st in first dc. (16)

Rnd 16: Ch2, dc2tog, dc1 in each stitch around, sl st in first dc. (15)

Rnd 17: Ch2, dc1 in each stitch around, sl st in first dc. (15)

Rnd 18: Ch2, dc2tog, dc1 in each stitch around, sl st in first dc. (14)

Rnd 19: Ch2, dc1 in each stitch around, sl st in first dc. (14)

Rnd 20: Ch2, dc2tog, dc1 in each stitch around, sl st in first dc. (13)

Rnd 21: Ch2, dc1 in each stitch around, sl st in first dc. (13)

Rnd 22: Ch2, dc2tog, dc1 in each stitch around, sl st in first dc. (12)

Cut a long tail to attach arms to body later.

LEGS (MAKE 2)

Repeat instructions for arms from rnd 1 up to
and including rnd 14.

Cut yarn and weave in ends.

PUTTING IT ALL TOGETHER

- Stuff the arms and legs very lightly, just enough to keep them from falling flat. If you're worried the stuffing will come through the double crocheted pieces, you can put the stuffing in a piece of tights or netting.
- Take the body and place both legs between the bottom two layers. With the remaining yarn from the body, sew across the seam with the legs in between. This way you close the bottom and assemble pieces at the same time.
- Sew an arm to each side of the body between rnds 1 and 3.
- Sew rnd 18 of the head to rnd 1 of the body.

BABY SLOTH

DIFFICULTY LEVEL: 3 of 5

SIZE: 5 in (13 cm) tall

MATERIALS

Yarn: DK #3 light weight yarn; shown in Scheepjes Stone Washed
- White (Moon Stone 801): 33 yd (30 m)
- Beige (Boulder Opal 804): 109.5 yd (100 m)
- Brown (Brown Agate 822): 22 yd (20 m)

Crochet hook: US size D-3 (3 mm)

Other:
- Brown and black safety eyes, 12 mm
- Fiberfill stuffing
- Needle and scissors

RIGHT EYE

Rnd 1: With brown, start with a magic loop, 6sc in the loop. (6) Don't pull loop too tight, so safety eye can fit through.

Rnd 2: Sl st, ch2, 2dc in same as previous sl st, hdc1, sc1, sl st (you won't work each stitch in this rnd).

Cut a long tail, insert safety eye in center of magic loop, but don't secure yet! Continue with left eye.

LEFT EYE

Rnd 1: With brown, start with a magic loop, 6sc in the loop. (6) Don't pull loop too tight, so safety eye can fit through.

Rnd 2: Sc1, hdc1, 2dc in next, ch2, sl st in same as previous dc (you won't work each stitch in this rnd).

Cut a long tail, insert safety eye in center of magic loop, but don't secure yet! Continue with nose.

NOSE

Rnd 1: With brown, start with a magic loop, sc1, dc1, sc2, dc1, sc1, sl st in first sc. (6)

Cut a long tail and continue with head.

HEAD

Rnd 1: With white, start with a magic loop, 6sc in the loop. (6)
Rnd 2: 2sc in each stitch around. (12)
Rnd 3: *Sc1, 2sc in next stitch*, repeat around. (18)
Rnd 4: *Sc2, 2sc in next stitch*, repeat around. (24)
Rnd 5: *Sc3, 2sc in next stitch*, repeat around. (30)
Rnd 6: Continue with beige (cut the white yarn), *sc4, 2sc in next stitch*, repeat around. (36)
Rnd 7: *Sc5, 2sc in next stitch*, repeat around. (42)
Rnds 8–9: Sc1 in each stitch around. (42)
Rnd 10: *Sc5, sc2tog*, repeat around. (36)
Rnd 11: *Sc4, sc2tog*, repeat around. (30)
Rnd 12: *Sc3, sc2tog*, repeat around. (24)
Rnd 13: *Sc2, sc2tog*, repeat around. (18)

Place the eyes between rnds 2 and 6 on both sides of the head, in the corner over the color change. Secure safety eyes through both layers and sew eyes in place with remaining yarn. Take the nose and with the dcs on each side place between the eyes and sew in place (the bottom should be a bit lower than the eyes). Stuff the head firmly.

Rnd 14: *Sc1, sc2tog*, repeat around. (12)
Rnd 15: *Sc2tog*, repeat around (6)

Cut a long tail, weave through the 6 remaining stitches, pull tight, and leave the end to sew the head to the body later.

BODY

Rnd 1: With beige, ch13, dc1 in 3rd ch from hook, dc9, 3dc in last, continue along the other side of the chains, dc10, 3dc in last, sl st in first dc. (26)

Rnd 2: Ch2 (doesn't count as first stitch now and throughout), *dc12, 2dc in next*, repeat one more time, sl st in first dc. (28)
Rnd 3: Ch2, *dc13, 2dc in next*, repeat one more time, sl st in first dc. (30)
Rnd 4: Ch2, *dc14, 2dc in next*, repeat one more time, sl st in first dc. (32)
Rnd 5: Ch2, *dc15, 2dc in next*, repeat one more time, sl st in first dc. (34)
Rnd 6: Ch2, *dc16, 2dc in next*, repeat one more time, sl st in first dc. (36)
Rnd 7: Ch2, *dc17, 2dc in next*, repeat one more time, sl st in first dc. (38)
Rnd 8: Ch2, *dc18, 2dc in next*, repeat one more time, sl st in first dc. (40)
Rnd 9: Ch2, *dc19, 2dc in next*, repeat one more time, sl st in first dc. (42)
Rnd 10: Ch2, *dc20, ch14, dc1 in 3rd ch from hook, dc1 in each of the remaining 11 chains, 2dc in next dc of rnd 9*, repeat one more time, sl st in first dc.

Cut a long tail to close the body later.

ARMS (MAKE 2)

Rnd 1: With beige, start with a magic loop, 6sc in the loop. (6)
Rnd 2: 2sc in each stitch around. (12)
Rnd 3: *Sc1, 2sc in next stitch*, repeat around. (18)
Rnd 4: *With beige: sc1, with white: dc3tog in 1 stitch (to make a bobble)*, repeat from * to * 2 more times; continue with beige (cut the white yarn), sc12. (18)

Note: The dc3tog-bobble tends to fall to the inside, so make sure to pop them to the outside.

Rnd 5: Sc1 in each stitch around. (18)
Rnd 6: *Sc1, sc2tog*, repeat around. (12)
Rnd 7: Sc1 in each stitch around. (12)

Rnd 8: Sl st 1, ch2 (doesn't count as first dc now and throughout), dc1 in each stitch around, sl st in first dc. (12)

Stuff the hand.

Rnd 9: Ch2, dc2tog, dc1 in each stitch around, sl st in first dc. (11)

Rnd 10: Ch2, dc1 in each stitch around, sl st in first dc. (11)

Rnd 11: Ch2, dc2tog, dc1 in each stitch around, sl st in first dc. (10)

Rnd 12: Ch2, dc1 in each stitch around, sl st in first dc. (10)

Rnd 13: Ch2, dc2tog, dc1 in each stitch around, sl st in first dc. (9)

Stuff the arm very lightly and cut a long tail to attach arms later.

PUTTING IT ALL TOGETHER

- Fold the body in line with the increases to make the belly straight and sew closed with the remaining yarn. Tie a knot in the corners to form the feet.
- Sew an arm to each side of the body between rnds 1 and 2.
- Finally, sew the bottom of rnd 11 of the head to rnd 1 of the body.

MATRYOSHKA

DIFFICULTY LEVEL: 4 of 5

SIZE: 12 in (30 cm) tall

MATERIALS

Yarn: DK #3 light weight yarn;
shown in Scheepjes Stone
Washed
- Light blue (Amazonite
  813): 109.5 yd (100 m)
- Red (Carnelian 823):
  87.5 yd (80 m)
- Light pink (Pink Quartz-
  ite 821): 76.5 yd (70 m)
- Pink (Rose Quartz 820):
  54.5 yd (50 m)
- Brown (Brown Agate
  822): 54.5 yd (50 m)

Crochet hook: US size D-3
(3 mm)

Other:
- Black and blue safety
  eyes, 15 mm
- Fiberfill stuffing
- Needle and scissors

HAIR AND HEAD

Rnd 1: With brown, start with a magic loop, 6sc in
the loop. (6)
Rnd 2: 2sc in each stitch around. (12)
Rnd 3: *Sc1, 2sc in next*, repeat around. (18)
Rnd 4: *Sc2, 2sc in next*, repeat around. (24)
Rnd 5: *Sc3, 2sc in next*, repeat around. (30)
Rnd 6: *Sc4, 2sc in next*, repeat around. (36)
Rnd 7: *Sc5, 2sc in next*, repeat around. (42)
Rnd 8: *Sc6, 2sc in next*, repeat around. (48)
Rnds 9–12: Sc1 in each stitch around. (48)
Rnd 13: Sc17, with light pink: sc1, with brown: sc30.
(48)
Rnd 14: Sc17, with light pink: sc3, with brown:
sc28. (48)
Rnd 15: Sc17, with light pink: sc5, with brown:
sc26. (48)
Rnd 16: Sc16, with light pink: sc8, with brown:
sc24. (48)
Rnd 17: Sc15, with light pink: sc11, with brown:
sc22. (48)
Rnd 18: Sc14, with light pink: sc14, with brown:
sc20. (48)
Rnd 19: Sc13, with light pink: sc17, with brown:
sc18. (48)
Rnd 20: Sc12, with light pink: sc20, with brown:
sc16. (48)
Rnd 21: Sc11, with light pink: sc23, with brown:
sc14. (48)
Rnd 22: Sc10, with light pink: sc38. (48)

Cut the brown yarn.

Rnd 23: *Sc6, sc2tog*, repeat around. (42)
Rnd 24: *Sc5, sc2tog*, repeat around. (36)
Rnd 25: *Sc4, sc2tog*, repeat around. (30)
Rnd 26: *Sc3, sc2tog*, repeat around. (24)
Rnd 27: *Sc2, sc2tog*, repeat around. (18)

Attach eyes between rnds 20 and 21, with 10 stitches between them, and stuff the head.

Rnd 28: *Sc1, sc2tog*, repeat around. (12)

Cut a long tail, fold the opening horizontally, and sew the seam closed.

BODY

Rnd 1: With light blue, ch18, 1dc in 3rd ch from hook, dc14, 3dc in last, continue along other side of chain, dc15, 3dc in last, sl st in first dc. (36)
Rnd 2: Ch2 (doesn't count as first dc now and throughout), *dc17, 2dc in next*, repeat one more time, sl st in first dc. (38)
Rnd 3: Ch2, *dc18, 2dc in next*, repeat one more time, sl st in first dc. (40)
Rnd 4: Ch2, *dc19, 2dc in next*, repeat one more time, sl st in first dc. (42)
Rnd 5: Ch2, *dc20, 2dc in next*, repeat one more time, sl st in first dc. (44)
Rnd 6: Ch2, *dc21, 2dc in next*, repeat one more time, sl st in first dc. (46)
Rnd 7: Ch2, *dc22, 2dc in next*, repeat one more time, sl st in first dc. (48)
Rnd 8: Ch2, *dc23, 2dc in next*, repeat one more time, sl st in first dc. (50)
Rnd 9: Ch2, *dc24, 2dc in next*, repeat one more time, sl st in first dc. (52)
Rnd 10: Ch2, *dc25, 2dc in next*, repeat one more time, sl st in first dc. (54)
Rnd 11: Ch1 (doesn't count as first sc now and throughout), sc3, ch20, skip 20 dc (pocket), sc1 in each of the remaining stitches. (54)

Rnd 12: Ch2, *dc26, 2dc in next*, repeat one more time, sl st in first dc. (56)
Rnd 13: Ch2, *dc27, 2dc in next*, repeat one more time, sl st in first dc. (58)
Rnd 14: Ch2, *dc28, 2dc in next*, repeat one more time, sl st in first dc. (60)
Rnd 15: Ch2, *dc8, dc2tog*, repeat around, sl st in first dc. (54)
Rnd 16: Ch2, *dc7, dc2tog*, repeat around, sl st in first dc. (48)
Rnd 17: Ch2, *dc6, dc2tog*, repeat around, sl st in first dc. (42)
Rnd 18: Ch2, *dc5, dc2tog*, repeat around, sl st in first dc. (36)
Rnd 19: Ch2, *dc4, dc2tog*, repeat around, sl st in first dc. (30)
Rnd 20: Ch2, *dc3, dc2tog*, repeat around, sl st in first dc. (24)
Rnd 21: Ch2, *dc2, dc2tog*, repeat around, sl st in first dc. (18)
Rnd 22: Ch2, *dc1, dc2tog*, repeat around, sl st in first dc. (12)

Cut a long tail to close the body, fold the body in line with the increases to make the belly straight, weave the yarn end through the 12 remaining stitches, and pull tight.

EMBELLISHING THE BODY

With rnd 1 toward you and the bottom facing away, attach red yarn to the first ch of rnd 11.

Row 1: Ch1 (doesn't count as first sc), sc20. (20)
Row 2: Turn, ch1, sc1, *sc1, 2dc in next stitch, sl st 1*, repeat from * to * 5 more times, sl st 1. (20)

Cut yarn and weave in ends.

FLOWER (MAKE 2)

Rnd 1: With red or pink, start with a magic loop, 5sc in the loop. (5)
Rnd 2: Continue with pink or red (cut the other color of yarn and weave in end), *in next stitch:

scl, dc2, sl st 1*, repeat 4 more times, sl st in first sc. (5 petals)

Cut yarn and sew to the body of the matryoshka.

ARMS (MAKE 2)

Rnd 1: With pink color, start with a magic loop, 6sc in the loop. (6)
Rnd 2: 2sc in each stitch around. (12)
Rnd 3: *Scl, 2sc in next*, repeat around. (18)
Rnds 4–10: Scl in each stitch around. (18)

Cut a long tail; you'll use it after rnd 12.

Rnd 11: With red, sl st 1, ch2 (doesn't count as first stitch now and throughout), dcl in each stitch around, sl st in first dc. (18)
Rnd 12: With light pink (cut the red yarn), ch2, dc2tog, dcl in each stitch around, sl st in first dc. (17)

At this point, stuff the hand. Take the remaining light pink yarn and sew across the arm between rnds 10 and 11.

Rnd 13: Ch2, dcl in each stitch around, sl st in first dc. (17)
Rnd 14: Ch2, dc2tog, dcl in each stitch around, sl st in first dc. (16)
Rnd 15: Ch2, dcl in each stitch around, sl st in first dc. (16)

Rnd 16: Ch2, dc2tog, dcl in each stitch around, sl st in first dc. (15)
Rnd 17: Ch2, dcl in each stitch around, sl st in first dc. (15)
Rnd 18: Ch2, dc2tog, dcl in each stitch around, sl st in first dc. (14)
Rnd 19: Ch2, dcl in each stitch around, sl st in first dc. (14)

Cut a long tail to attach arms to body later.

HOOD

Row 1: With red, ch30, scl in second ch from hook, sc28. (30)
Rows 2–30: Turn, chl (counts as first sc from now on), sc29. (30)

Fold the hood in half, so the two halves of the starting chains are against each other, and sew them together. Fit the hood to be sure it's the right size; it should cover the top of the body too. If it's too short you can simply add a few rows. Once you're sure it's long enough, cut a long tail to sew the hood in place later.

Row 31: With pink, sl st in first sc, *dcl, sl st 1*, repeat to last sc, cut yarn, and weave in ends.

PUTTING IT ALL TOGETHER

- Sew the back of rnd 25 of the head to rnd 1 of the body.
- Sew an arm to each side of the body between rnds 1 and 3.
- Place the hood on the head, gather it under the chin, and sew in place; the bottom stays open.
- Sew the hood to the head along the opening around the face.

BABY MATRYOSHKA

DIFFICULTY LEVEL: 3 of 5

SIZE: 4.5 in (12 cm) tall

MATERIALS

Yarn: DK #3 light weight yarn; shown in Scheepjes Stone Washed

- Pink (Rose Quartz 820): 65.5 yd (60 m)
- Brown (Brown Agate 822): 54.5 yd (50 m)
- Light pink (Pink Quartzite 821): 44 yd (40 m)
- Lilac (Lilac Quartz 818): 44 yd (40 m)
- Turquoise (Green Agate 815): 22 yd (20 m)

Crochet hook: US size D-3 (3 mm)

Other:
- Black and blue safety eyes, 8 mm
- Fiberfill stuffing
- Needle and scissors

HAIR AND HEAD

Rnd 1: With brown, start with a magic loop, 6sc in the loop. (6)

Rnd 2: 2sc in each stitch around. (12)

Rnd 3: *Sc1, 2sc in next*, repeat around. (18)

Rnd 4: *Sc2, 2sc in next*, repeat around. (24)

Rnd 5: Sc1 in each stitch around. (24)

Rnd 6: Sc7, with light pink: sc1, with brown: sc16. (24)

Rnd 7: Sc7, with light pink: sc3, with brown: sc14. (24)

Rnd 8: Sc6, with light pink: sc6, with brown: sc12. (24)

Rnd 9: Sc6, with light pink: sc7, with brown: sc11. (24)

Rnd 10: Sc6, with light pink: sc8, with brown: sc10. (24)

Rnd 11: Sc6, with light pink: sc9, with brown: sc9. (24)

Rnd 12: Sc6, with light pink: sc18; you can cut the brown yarn. (24)

Rnd 13: *Sc2, sc2tog*, repeat around. (18)

Attach eyes between rnds 9 and 10, with 5 stitches between them, and stuff the head.

Rnd 14: *Sc1, sc2tog*, repeat around. (12)

Cut a long tail, fold the opening horizontally, and sew the seam closed.

BODY

Rnd 1: With pink, ch10, dc1 in 3rd ch from hook, dc6, 3dc in last, continue along the other side of the chains, dc7, 3dc in last, sl st in first dc. (20)

Rnd 2: Ch2 (doesn't count as first stitch now and throughout), *dc9, 2dc in next*, repeat one more time, sl st in first dc. (22)

Rnd 3: Ch2, *dc10, 2dc in next*, repeat one more time, sl st in first dc. (24)

Rnd 4: Ch2, *dc11, 2dc in next*, repeat one more time, sl st in first dc. (26)

Rnd 5: Ch2, *dc12, 2dc in next*, repeat one more time, sl st in first dc. (28)

Rnd 6: Ch2, *dc13, 2dc in next*, repeat one more time, sl st in first dc. (30)

Rnd 7: Ch2, *dc3, dc2tog*, repeat around, sl st in first dc. (24)

Rnd 8: Ch2, *dc2, dc2tog*, repeat around, sl st in first dc. (18)

Rnd 9: Ch2, *dc1, dc2tog*, repeat around, sl st in first dc. (12)

Cut a long tail to close the body, fold the body in line with the increases to make the belly straight, weave the yarn end through the 12 remaining stitches, pull tight, and sew in place.

FLOWER

Rnd 1: With turquoise, start with a magic loop, 5sc in the loop. (5)

PUTTING IT ALL TOGETHER

- Sew the back of rnd 12 of the head to rnd 1 of the body.
- Place the hood on the head, gather it under the chin, and sew in place; the bottom stays open.
- Sew the hood to the head along the opening around the face.

Rnd 2: Continue with lilac (cut the turquoise yarn and weave in end), *in next stitch: sc1, dc2, sl st 1*, repeat 4 more times, sl st in first sc. (5 petals)

Cut yarn and sew to the body of the matryoshka.

HOOD

Row 1: With lilac, ch17, sc1 in second ch from hook, sc15. (17)

Rows 2–18: Turn, ch1 (counts as first sc from now on), sc16. (17)

Fold the hood in half, so the two halves of the starting chains are against each other, and sew them together. Fit the hood to be sure it's the right size; it should cover the top of the body too. If it's too short you can simply add a few rows. Once you're sure it's long enough, cut a long tail to sew the hood in place later.

Row 19: With turquoise, sl st in first sc, *dc1, sl st 1*, repeat to last sc, cut chin, and weave in ends.

Baby fits in the Matryoshka's pocket.

DUTCH FARM GIRL

DIFFICULTY LEVEL: 5 of 5

SIZE: 12 in (30 cm) tall

MATERIALS

Yarn: DK #3 light weight yarn; shown in Scheepjes Stone Washed
- Light blue (Amazonite 813): 87.5 yd (80 m)
- Yellow (Yellow Jasper 809): 87.5 yd (80 m)
- White (Moon Stone 801): 65.5 yd (60 m)
- Light pink (Pink Quartzite 821): 54.5 yd (50 m)
- Dark blue (Blue Apatite 805): 54.5 yd (50 m)
- Red (Carnelian 823): 22 yd (20 m)

Crochet hook: US size D-3 (3 mm)

Other:
- Black and blue safety eyes, 12 mm
- Fiberfill stuffing
- Yarn needle and scissors

HEAD

Rnd 1: With yellow, start with a magic ring, 6sc in the ring. (6)

Rnd 2: 2sc in each stitch around. (12)

Rnd 3: *Sc1, 2sc in next*, repeat around. (18)

Rnd 4: *Sc2, 2sc in next*, repeat around. (24)

Rnd 5: *Sc3, 2sc in next*, repeat around. (30)

Rnd 6: *Sc4, 2sc in next*, repeat around. (36)

Rnd 7: *Sc5, 2sc in next*, repeat around. (42)

Rnd 8: *Sc6, 2sc in next*, repeat around. (48)

Rnds 9–12: Sc1 in each stitch around. (48)

Rnd 13: With yellow: sc15, with light pink: sc1, with yellow: sc32. (48)

Rnd 14: With yellow: sc15, with light pink: sc3, with yellow: sc30. (48)

Rnd 15: With yellow: sc15, with light pink: sc5, with yellow: sc28. (48)

Rnd 16: With yellow: sc14, with light pink: sc8, with yellow: sc26. (48)

Rnd 17: With yellow: sc13, with light pink: sc11, with yellow: sc24. (48)

Rnd 18: With yellow: sc12, with light pink: sc14, with yellow: sc22. (48)

Rnd 19: With yellow: sc11, with light pink: sc17, with yellow: sc20. (48)

Rnd 20: With yellow: sc10, with light pink: sc20, with yellow: sc18. (48)

Rnd 21: With yellow: sc9, with light pink: sc23, with yellow: sc16. (48)

Rnd 22: With yellow: sc8, with light pink: sc40. (48)

Cut the yellow yarn.

Rnd 23: *Sc6, sc2tog*, repeat around. (42)
Rnd 24: *Sc5, sc2tog*, repeat around. (36)
Rnd 25: *Sc4, sc2tog*, repeat around. (30)
Rnd 26: *Sc3, sc2tog*, repeat around. (24)
Rnd 27: *Sc2, sc2tog*, repeat around. (18)

Attach safety eyes between rnds 19 and 20 of head, 10 stitches apart, and stuff the head.

Rnd 28: *Sc1, sc2tog*, repeat around. (12)

Cut a long tail and sew the bottom seam closed.

HAT

Rnd 1: With white: start with a magic ring, 6sc in the ring. (6)
Rnd 2: Sc1 in each stitch around. (6)
Rnd 3: 2sc in each stitch around. (12)
Rnd 4: Sc1 in each stitch around. (12)
Rnd 5: *Sc1, 2sc in next*, repeat around. (18)
Rnd 6: Sc1 in each stitch around. (18)
Rnd 7: *Sc2, 2sc in next*, repeat around. (24)
Rnd 8: Sc1 in each stitch around. (24)
Rnd 9: *Sc3, 2sc in next*, repeat around. (30)
Rnd 10: Sc1 in each stitch around. (30)
Rnd 11: *Sc4, 2sc in next*, repeat around. (36)
Rnd 12: Sc1 in each stitch around. (36)
Rnd 13: *Sc5, 2sc in next*, repeat around. (42)

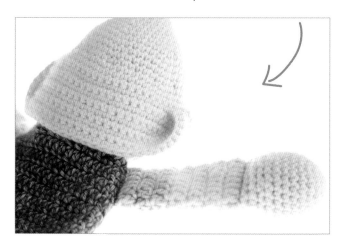

Rnd 14: Sc1 in each stitch around. (42)
Rnd 15: *Sc6, 2sc in next*, repeat around. (48)
Rnd 16: Sc1 in each stitch around. (48)
Rnd 17: *Sc7, 2sc in next*, repeat around. (54)
Rnd 18: Sc1 in each stitch around. (54)
Rnd 19: Sc42, from now on you'll crochet from side to side instead of in the round. (42)
Rows 20–29: Ch1 (counts as first sc from now on), turn, sc41. (42)

Place the hat on the head, slightly tilted to the back so the back of the neck is completely covered. Leave a long tail, sew rnd 18 of the hat to rnd 11 of the head all around; the bottom of the hat isn't sewn on.

BODY

Rnd 1: With dark blue, ch18, 1dc in 3rd ch from hook, dc14, 3dc in last, continue along the other side of the chains, dc15, 3dc in last, sl st in first dc. (36)
Rnd 2: Ch2 (doesn't count as first stitch now and throughout), *dc17, 2dc in next*, repeat one more time, sl st in first dc. (38)
Rnd 3: Ch2, *dc18, 2dc in next*, repeat one more time, sl st in first dc. (40)
Rnd 4: Ch2, *dc19, 2dc in next*, repeat one more time, sl st in first dc. (42)
Rnd 5: Ch2, *dc20, 2dc in next*, repeat one more time, sl st in first dc. (44)
Rnd 6: Ch2, *dc21, 2dc in next*, repeat one more time, sl st in first dc. (46)
Rnd 7: Ch2, *dc22, 2dc in next*, repeat one more time, sl st in first dc. (48)
Rnd 8: Ch2, *dc23, 2dc in next*, repeat one more time, sl st in first dc. (50)
Rnd 9: Ch2, *dc24, 2dc in next*, repeat one more time, sl st in first dc. (52)

Cut the blue yarn.

Rnd 10: With white: ch2, *dc25, 2dc in next*, repeat one more time, sl st in first dc. (54)

Cut the white yarn.

Rnd 11: With light blue, in back loops only, ch2, *dc26, 2dc in next*, repeat one more time, sl st in first dc. (56)

Rnd 12: Ch2, *dc27, 2dc in next*, repeat one more time, sl st in first dc. (58)

Rnd 13: Ch2, *dc28, 2dc in next*, repeat one more time, sl st in first dc. (60)

Rnd 14: Ch2, *dc29, 2dc in next*, repeat one more time, sl st in first dc. (62)

Rnd 15: Ch2, *dc30, 2dc in next*, repeat one more time, sl st in first dc. (64)

Rnd 16: Ch2, *dc31, 2dc in next*, repeat one more time, sl st in first dc. (66)

Rnd 17: Ch2, *dc32, 2dc in next*, repeat one more time, sl st in first dc. (68)

Rnd 18: Ch2, *dc33, 2dc in next*, repeat one more time, sl st in first dc. (70)

Rnd 19: For this row you'll alternate colors every stitch: the color pattern is 1 stitch red, 1 stitch white, and 1 stitch dark blue. I keep the yarn of the colors I don't use just hanging in the back and pick them up 2 stitches later again. Ch2, *dc34, 2dc in next*, repeat one more time, sl st in first dc. (72)

Rnd 20: Ch2, *dc35, 2dc in next*, repeat one more time, sl st in first dc. (74)

Rnd 21: Ch2, *dc36, 2dc in next*, repeat one more time, sl st in first dc. (76)

Cut a long tail to close the body later. Fold the body in line with the increases to make the belly straight.

ARMS (MAKE 2)

Rnd 1: With light pink: start with a magic loop, 6sc in the loop. (6)

Rnd 2: 2sc in each stitch around. (12)

Rnd 3: *Sc1, 2sc in next*, repeat around. (18)

Rnd 4: *Sc2, 2sc in next*, repeat around. (24)

Rnds 5–9: Sc1 in each stitch around. (24)

Rnd 10: *Sc2, sc2tog*, repeat around. (18)

Rnds 11–12: Sc1 in each stitch around. (18)

Rnd 13: Sl st 1, ch2 (doesn't count as first stitch now and throughout), dc in each stitch around, sl st in first dc. (18)

Rnd 14: Ch2, dc2tog, dc in each stitch around, sl st in first dc. (17)

At this point, stuff the hand. Take a little piece of light pink yarn and sew across the arm between rnds 12 and 13.

Rnd 15: Ch2, dc in each stitch around, sl st in first dc. (17)

Rnd 16: Ch2, dc2tog, dc in each stitch around, sl st in first dc. (16)

Cut the light pink yarn.

Rnd 17: With light blue: ch2, dc in each stitch around, sl st in first dc. (16)

Rnd 18: Ch2, dc2tog, dc in each stitch around, sl st in first dc. (15)

Rnd 19: Ch2, dc in each stitch around, sl st in first dc. (15)

Cut a long tail to attach arms to body later.

CLOGS (MAKE 2)

Rnd 1: With yellow: start with a magic loop, 6sc in the loop. (6)

Rnd 2: 2sc in each stitch around. (12)

Rnd 3: *Sc1, 2sc in next*, repeat around. (18)

Rnd 4: *Sc2, 2sc in next*, repeat around. (24)

Rnds 5 to 6: Sc1 in each stitch around. (24)

Rnd 7: Sc10, sc4tog, sc10. (21)

Rnd 8: Sc8, sc5tog, sc8. (17)

Rnd 9: Sl st 1, ch2 (doesn't count as first stitch now and throughout), dc in each stitch around, sl st in first dc. (17)

Cut a long tail, stuff the bottom part of the clog, and sew across the clog between rnds 8 and 9.

APRON

Row 1: For this row you'll alternate colors every stitch: the color pattern is 1 stitch white, 1 stitch red. Lay the body in front of you upside down, and attach yarn in the 3rd unworked front loop of rnd 10, ch2 (doesn't count as first stitch now and throughout), dc21. (21)

Cut the red yarn.

Row 2: (Apron is worked from side to side instead of in the round.) With white, turn, ch2, dc3tog, dc15, dc3tog. (17)

Row 3: Turn, ch2, dc3tog, dc11, dc3tog. (13)

Row 4: Turn, ch2, dc3tog, dc7, dc3tog. (9)

Row 5: Turn, ch1 (does count as first stitch for this row), skip 1 stitch, 3dc in next stitch, dc3, 3dc in next stitch, skip 1 stitch, sl st in last.

Edging: With white: you'll work along the sides of each row, attach yarn in the side of row 1, ch1, *scl, ch3, sl st in first of 3 chains you just made*, repeat from * to * for each row until you reach the straight stitches of rnd 5, ^scl, ch3, sl st in first of 3 chains you just made, skip 1 stitch^, repeat from ^ to ^ to the end of row 5, then continue along the other side of the rows, scl, {ch3, sl st in first of 3 chains you just made, scl}, repeat from { to } to end. Cut yarn and weave in ends.

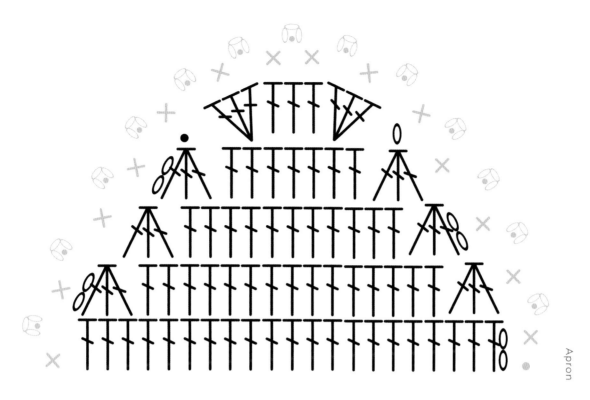

Apron

PUTTING IT ALL TOGETHER

- Take the body and place rnd 9 of both clogs between the bottom two layers. With remaining yarn from the body, sew across the seam with the clogs in between to close the bottom and assemble pieces at the same time.
- Sew an arm to each side of the body between rnds 1 and 3.
- Sew the back of rnd 23 of the head to rnd 1 of the body.

COW

DIFFICULTY LEVEL: 4 of 5

SIZE: 13.5 in (35 cm) tall

MATERIALS

Yarn: DK #3 light weight yarn; shown in Scheepjes Stone Washed
- Black (Black Onyx 803): 142 yd (130 m)
- White (Moon Stone 801): 142 yd (130 m)
- Pink (Rose Quartz 820): 87.5 yd (80 m)

Crochet hook: US size D-3 (3 mm)

Other:
- Black and gold safety eyes, 12 mm
- Fiberfill stuffing
- Yarn needle and scissors

EARS (MAKE 2)

Rnd 1: With black, start with a magic ring, 6sc in the ring. (6)
Rnd 2: Sc1 in each stitch around. (6)
Rnd 3: 2sc in each stitch around. (12)
Rnds 4–5: Sc1 in each stitch around. (12)
Rnd 6: *Sc1, 2sc in next*, repeat around. (18)
Rnd 7: Sc1 in each stitch around. (18)

Cut yarn and weave in ends.

HEAD

Rnd 1: With white, take first ear, sc1 in each of the 18 stitches of first ear, ch9, take second ear, sc1 in each of the 18 stitches of second ear, sc1 in each of the 9 chains you just made. (54)
Rnd 2: Sc1 in each stitch around. (54)
Rnd 3: Sc8, sc2tog, sc25, sc2tog, sc17. (52)
Rnd 4: Sc1 in each stitch around. (52)
Rnd 5: Sc8, sc2tog, sc24, sc2tog, sc16. (50)
Rnd 6: Sc1 in each stitch around. (50)
Rnd 7: Sc8, sc2tog, sc23, sc2tog, sc15. (48)
Rnd 8: Sc1 in each stitch around. (48)
Rnd 9: Sc8, sc2tog, sc22, sc2tog, sc14. (46)
Rnd 10: Sc1 in each stitch around. (46)
Rnd 11: Sc8, sc2tog, sc21, sc2tog, sc13. (44)
Rnd 12: Sc1 in each stitch around. (44)
Rnd 13: Sc8, sc2tog, sc20, sc2tog, sc12. (42)
Rnd 14: Sc1 in each stitch around. (42)

Rnd 15: Sc8, change to pink (you can cut the white yarn), sc1 in each stitch around. (42)

Rnds 16–22: Sc1 in each stitch around. (42)

Rnd 23: *Sc5, sc2tog*, repeat around. (36)

Rnd 24: *Sc4, sc2tog*, repeat around. (30)

Rnd 25: *Sc3, sc2tog*, repeat around (24)

Attach the safety eyes between rnds 9 and 10 of head, and stuff the ears and top part of the head.

Rnd 26: *Sc2, sc2tog*, repeat around. (18)

Stuff the rest of the head.

Rnd 27: *Sc1, sc2tog*, repeat around. (12)

Cut a long tail, and sew the seam of the mouth closed.

HORNS (MAKE 2)

Rnd 1: With white: start with a magic ring, 6sc in the ring. (6)

Rnd 2: Sc1 in each stitch around. (6)

Rnd 3: *Sc1, 2sc in next*, repeat around. (9)

Rnd 4: Sc1 in each stitch around. (9)

Rnd 5: *Sc2, 2sc in next*, repeat around. (12)

Rnd 6: Sc1 in each stitch around. (12)

Cut a long tail, stuff the horns, and sew to head next to the ear and slightly in front of it, next to the center on each side.

BODY

Rnd 1: With white: ch18, 1dc in 3rd ch from hook, dc14, 3dc in last, continue along other side of chains, dc15, 3dc in last, sl st in first dc. (36)

Rnd 2: With white: ch2 (doesn't count as first stitch now and throughout), *with white: dc12, with black: dc5, 2dc in next*, repeat one more time, sl st in first dc. (38)

Rnd 3: With white: ch2, *with white: dc3, with black: dc2, with white: dc5, with black: dc8, 2dc in next*, repeat one more time, sl st in first dc. (40)

Rnd 4: With white: ch2, *with white: dc3, with black: dc4, with white: dc5, with black: dc5, with white: dc2, 2dc in next*, repeat one more time, sl st in first dc. (42)

Rnd 5: With white: ch2, *with white: dc5, with black: dc5, with white: dc10, 2dc in next*, repeat one more time, sl st in first dc. (44)

Rnd 6: With black: ch2, *with black: dc3, with white: dc9, with black: dc3, with white: dc3, with black: dc3, 2dc in next*, repeat one more time, sl st in first dc. (46)

Rnd 7: With black: ch2, *with black: dc5, with white: dc5, with black: dc5, with white: dc3, with black: dc4, 2dc in next*, repeat one more time, sl st in first dc. (48)

Rnd 8: With black: ch2, *with black: dc7, with white: dc13, with black: dc3, 2dc in next*, repeat one more time, sl st in first dc. (50)

Rnd 9: With black: ch2, *with black: dc5, with white: dc19, 2dc in next*, repeat one more time, sl st in first dc. (52)

Rnd 10: With white: ch2, *with white: dc6, with black: dc3, with white: dc8, with black: dc5, with white: dc3, 2dc in next*, repeat one more time, sl st in first dc. (54)

Rnd 11: With black: ch2, *with black: dc2, with white: dc3, with black: dc6, with white: dc5, with black: dc8, with white: dc2, 2dc in next*, repeat one more time, sl st in first dc. (56)

Rnd 12: With black: ch2, *with black: dc3, with white: dc14, with black: dc7, with white: dc3, 2dc in next*, repeat one more time, sl st in first dc. (58)

Rnd 13: With black: ch2, *with black: dc5, with white: dc23, 2dc in next*, repeat one more time, sl st in first dc. (60)

Rnd 14: With black: ch2, *with black: dc7, with white: dc16, with black: dc3, with white: dc3, 2dc in next*, repeat one more time, sl st in first dc. (62)

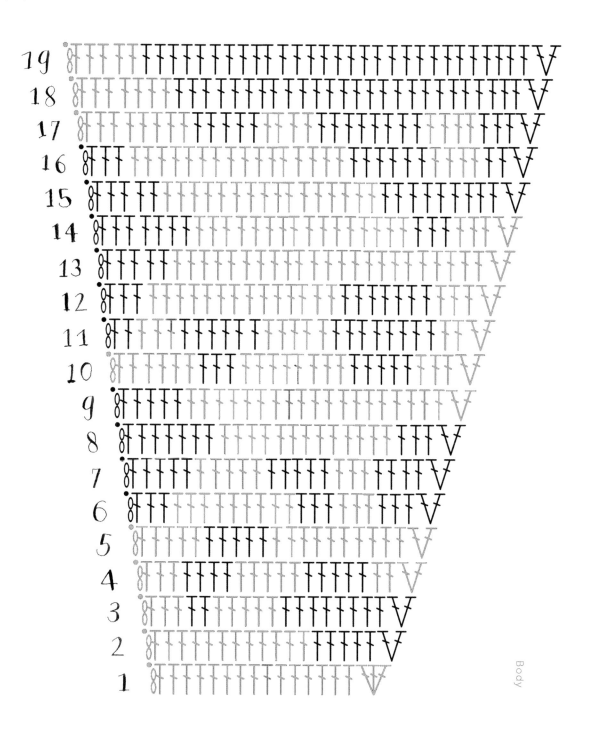

Body

Rnd 15: With black: ch2, *with black: dc5, with white: dc16, with black: dc9, 2dc in next*, repeat one more time, sl st in first dc. (64)

Rnd 16: With black: ch2, *with black: dc3, with white: dc16, with black: dc6, with white: dc4, with black: dc2, 2dc in next*, repeat one more time, sl st in first dc. (66)

Rnd 17: With white: ch2, *with white: dc8, with black: dc5, with white: dc4, with black: dc8, with white: dc4, with black: dc3, 2dc in next*, repeat one more time, sl st in first dc. (68)

Rnd 18: With white: ch2, *with white: dc7, with black: dc26, 2dc in next*, repeat one more time, sl st in first dc. (70)

Rnd 19: With white: ch2, *with white: dc5, with black: dc29, 2dc in next*, repeat one more time, sl st in first dc. (72)

ARMS (MAKE 2)

Rnd 1: With black: start with a magic loop, 6sc in the loop. (6)

Rnd 2: 2sc in each stitch around. (12)

Rnd 3: *Sc1, 2sc in next*, repeat around. (18)

Rnd 4: *Sc2, 2sc in next*, repeat around. (24)

Rnds 5–9: Sc1 in each stitch around. (24)

Rnd 10: *Sc2, sc2tog* repeat around. (18)

Rnds 11–12: Sc1 in each stitch around. (18)

Cut a long tail; you'll use it after rnd 14.

Rnd 13: With white: sl st 1, ch2 (doesn't count as first stitch now and throughout), dc in each stitch around, sl st in first dc. (18)

Rnd 14: Ch2, dc2tog, dc in each stitch around, sl st in first dc. (17)

At this point, stuff the hand. Take the remaining black yarn and sew across the arm between rnds 12 and 13.

Rnd 15: Ch2, dc in each stitch around, sl st in first dc. (17)

Rnd 16: Ch2, dc2tog, dc in each stitch around, sl st in first dc. (16)

Rnd 17: Ch2, dc in each stitch around, sl st in first dc. (16)

Rnd 18: Ch2, dc2tog, dc in each stitch around, sl st in first dc. (15)

Rnd 19: Ch2, dc in each stitch around, sl st in first dc. (15)

Rnd 20: Ch2, dc2tog, dc in each stitch around, sl st in first dc. (14)

Rnd 21: Ch2, dc in each stitch around, sl st in first dc. (14)

Rnd 22: Ch2, dc2tog, dc in each stitch around, sl st in first dc. (13)

Cut a long tail to attach arms to body later.

LEGS (MAKE 2)

Rnd 1: With black: start with a magic loop, ch2 (doesn't count as first dc), 12dc in the loop, sl st in first dc. (12)

Rnd 2: Ch2, *dc1, 2dc in next*, repeat around, sl st in first dc. (18)

Rnds 3–7: With white: ch2, dc in each stitch around, sl st in first dc. (18)

Cut yarn and weave in ends.

UDDER

Rnd 1: With pink: start with a magic loop, 6sc in the loop. (6)

Rnd 2: 2sc in each stitch around. (12)

Rnd 3: *Sc1, 2sc in next*, repeat around. (18)

Rnd 4: *Sc2, 2sc in next*, repeat around. (24)

Rnd 5: *Sc3, 2sc in next*, repeat around. (30)

Rnd 6: *Sc4, 2sc in next*, repeat around. (36)

Rnd 7: *Sc8, 8dc in next stitch*, repeat around. (64)

Rnd 8: *Sc8, dc8tog*, repeat around. (36)

Rnd 9: Sc1 in each stitch around. (36)

Stuff the udder and sew to the body between rnds 13 and 17.

PUTTING IT ALL TOGETHER

- Take the body and place both legs between the bottom two layers. With the remaining yarn from the body, sew across the seam with the legs in between. This way you close the bottom and assemble pieces at the same time.
- Sew an arm to each side of the body between rnds 1 and 3.
- Sew rnd 16 of the head (ears not included) to rnd 1 of the body.

BABY COW

DIFFICULTY LEVEL: 4 of 5

SIZE: 7 in (18 cm) tall

MATERIALS

Yarn: DK #3 light weight yarn; shown in Scheepjes Stone Washed
- Black (Black Onyx 803): 87.5 yd (80 m)
- White (Moon Stone 801): 87.5 yd (80 m)
- Pink (Rose Quartz 820): 54.5 yd (50 m)

Crochet hook: US size D-3 (3 mm)

Other:
- Black and gold safety eyes, 8 mm
- Fiberfill stuffing
- Yarn needle and scissors

EARS (MAKE 2)

Rnd 1: With black: start with a magic ring, 6sc in the ring. (6)
Rnd 2: Sc1 in each stitch around. (6)
Rnd 3: 2sc in each stitch around. (12)
Rnds 4–5: Sc1 in each stitch around. (12)

Cut yarn and weave in ends.

HEAD

Rnd 1: With white: take first ear, sc1 in each of the 12 stitches of first ear, ch6, take second ear, sc1 in each of the 12 stitches of second ear, sc1 in each of the 6 chains you just made. (36)
Rnd 2: Sc1 in each stitch around. (36)
Rnd 3: Sc4, sc2tog, sc16, sc2tog, sc12. (34)
Rnd 4: Sc4, sc2tog, sc15, sc2tog, sc11. (32)
Rnd 5: Sc4, sc2tog, sc14, sc2tog, sc10. (30)
Rnd 6: Sc4, sc2tog, sc13, sc2tog, sc9. (28)
Rnd 7: Sc4, sc2tog, sc12, sc2tog, sc8. (26)
Rnd 8: Sc4, sc2tog, sc11, sc2tog, sc7. (24)
Rnd 9: Sc4, change to pink (you can cut the white yarn), sc1 in each stitch around. (24)
Rnds 10–13: Sc1 in each stitch around. (24)

Attach safety eyes between rnds 6 and 7 of the head (ears not included).

Rnd 14: *Sc2, sc2tog*, repeat around. (18)

Stuff the head and ears.

Rnd 15: *Sc1, sc2tog*, repeat around. (12)
Rnd 16: *Sc2tog*, repeat around. (6)

Cut a long tail, and sew the seam of the mouth closed.

HORNS (MAKE 2)

Rnd 1: With white: start with a magic ring, 6sc in the ring. (6)
Rnds 2–3: Sc1 in each stitch around. (6)

Cut a long tail, sew to head next to the ear and slightly in front of it, next to the center on each side.

BODY

Rnd 1: With white: ch13, 1dc in 3rd ch from hook, dc9, 3dc in last, continue along other side of chains, dc10, 3dc in last, sl st in first dc. (26)
Rnd 2: With black: ch2 (doesn't count as first stitch now and throughout), *with black: dc6, with white: dc3, with black: dc2, with white: dc1, 2dc in next*, repeat one more time, sl st in first dc. (28)
Rnd 3: With black: ch2, *with black: dc4, with white: dc5, with black: dc3, with white: dc1, 2dc in next*, repeat one more time, sl st in first dc. (30)
Rnd 4: With white: ch2, *dc14, 2dc in next*, repeat one more time, sl st in first dc. (32)
Rnd 5: With white: ch2, *with white: dc2, with black: dc4, with white: dc6, with black: dc3, 2dc in next*, repeat one more time, sl st in first dc. (34)
Rnd 6: With white: ch2, *with white: dc1, with black: dc5, with white: dc5, with black: dc5, 2dc in next*, repeat one more time, sl st in first dc. (36)

Rnd 7: With white: ch2, *with white: dc3, with black: dc3, with white: dc6, with black: dc5, with white: 2dc in next*, repeat one more time, sl st in first dc. (38)
Rnd 8: With black: ch2, *with black: dc3, with white: dc5, with black: dc3, with white: dc7, 2dc in next*, repeat one more time, sl st in first dc. (40)
Rnd 9: With black: ch2, *with black: dc5, with white: dc11, with black: dc3, 2dc in next*, repeat one more time, sl st in first dc. (42)
Rnd 10: With black: ch2, *with black: dc3, with white: dc16, with black: dc1, 2dc in next*, repeat one more time, sl st in first dc. (44)
Rnd 11: With white: ch2, *with white: dc8, with black: dc6, with white: dc4, with black: dc3, 2dc in next*, repeat one more time, sl st in first dc. (46)
Rnd 12: With white: ch2, *with white: dc6, with black: dc7, with white: dc4, with black: dc5, ch14, dc1 in 3rd ch from hook, dc1 in each of the remaining 11 chains, 2dc in next stitch of rnd 11*, repeat one more time, sl st in first dc.

Cut a long tail to close the body later.

UDDER

Rnd 1: With pink: start with a magic loop, 6sc in the loop. (6)
Rnd 2: 2sc in each stitch around. (12)
Rnd 3: *Sc1, 2sc in next*, repeat around. (18)
Rnd 4: *Sc2, 2sc in next*, repeat around. (24)
Rnd 5: *Sc5, 6dc in next stitch*, repeat around. (44)
Rnd 6: *Sc5, dc6tog*, repeat around. (24)
Rnd 7: Sc1 in each stitch around. (24)

Stuff the udder and sew to the body between rnds 8 and 11.

ARMS (MAKE 2)

Rnd 1: With black: start with a magic loop, 6sc in the loop. (6)

Rnd 2: 2sc in each stitch around. (12)

Rnd 3: *Sc1, 2sc in next*, repeat around. (18)

Rnds 4–5: Sc1 in each stitch around. (18)

Rnd 6: *Sc1, sc2tog*, repeat around. (12)

Rnd 7: Sc1 in each stitch around. (12)

Cut a long tail; you'll use it after rnd 9.

Rnd 8: With white: sl st 1, ch2 (doesn't count as first stitch now and throughout), dc1 in each stitch around, sl st in first dc. (12)

Rnd 9: Ch2, dc2tog, dc1 in each stitch around, sl st in first dc. (11)

At this point, stuff the hand. Take the remaining black yarn and sew across the arm between rnds 7 and 8.

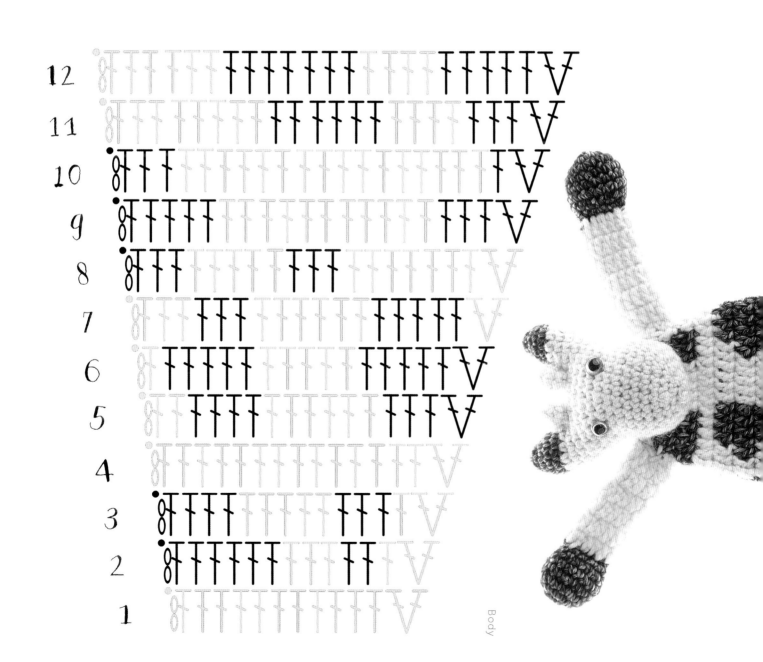

Body

Rnd 10: Ch2, dc1 in each stitch around, sl st in first dc. (11)

Rnd 11: Ch2, dc2tog, dc1 in each stitch around, sl st in first dc. (10)

Rnd 12: Ch2, dc1 in each stitch around, sl st in first dc. (10)

Rnd 13: Ch2, dc2tog, dc1 in each stitch around, sl st in first dc. (9)

Cut a long tail to attach arms to body later.

PUTTING IT ALL TOGETHER

- Take the head and sew rnd 8 of the head (ears not included) to rnd 1 of the body.
- Fold the body in line with the increases to make the belly straight and sew closed with the remaining yarn. Tie a knot in the corners to form the feet.
- Sew an arm to each side of the body in rnds 1 and 2.

KOALA

DIFFICULTY LEVEL: 2 of 5

SIZE: 12 in (30 cm)

MATERIALS

Yarn: DK #3 light weight yarn; shown in Scheepjes Stone Washed
- Light gray (Crystal Quartz 814): 197 yd (180 m)
- Black (Black Onyx 803): 54.5 yd (50 m)
- White (Moon Stone 801): 33 yd (30 m)

Crochet hook: US size D-3 (3 mm)

Other:
- Black safety eyes, 15 mm
- Fiberfill stuffing
- Needle and scissors

HEAD

Rnd 1: With light gray, start with a magic loop, 6sc in the loop. (6)

Rnd 2: 2sc in each stitch around. (12)

Rnd 3: *Sc1, 2sc in next*, repeat around. (18)

Rnd 4: *Sc2, 2sc in next*, repeat around. (24)

Rnd 5: *Sc3, 2sc in next*, repeat around. (30)

Rnd 6: *Sc4, 2sc in next*, repeat around. (36)

Rnd 7: *Sc5, 2sc in next*, repeat around. (42)

Rnd 8: *Sc6, 2sc in next*, repeat around. (48)

Rnd 9: *Sc7, 2sc in next*, repeat around. (54)

Rnds 10–17: Sc1 in each stitch around. (54)

Rnd 18: *Sc7, sc2tog*, repeat around. (48)

Rnd 19: *Sc6, sc2tog*, repeat around. (42)

Rnd 20: *Sc5, sc2tog*, repeat around. (36)

Rnd 21: *Sc4, sc2tog*, repeat around. (30)

Rnd 22: *Sc3, sc2tog*, repeat around. (24)

Rnd 23: *Sc2, sc2tog*, repeat around. (18)

At this point, attach safety eyes between rnds 16 and 17, 10 stitches apart, and stuff the head.

Rnd 24: *Sc1, sc2tog*, repeat around. (12)

Rnd 25: *Sc2tog*, repeat around. (6)

Cut yarn, weave through remaining stitches, pull tight, and weave in end.

NOSE

Rnd 1: With black: start with a magic loop, 6sc in the loop. (6)
Rnd 2: 2sc in first stitch, 2hdc in next stitch, 2dc in next stitch, 2hdc in next stitch, 2sc in each of the last 2 stitches. (12)
Rnd 3: Sc1, 2sc in next stitch, sc1, 2sc in next stitch, 2hdc in next stitch, 2dc in each of the next 2 stitches, 2hdc in next stitch, sc1, 2sc in next stitch, sc1, 2sc in next stitch. (20)

Cut a long tail and sew nose to head, centered between the eyes, from rnd 13 to rnd 20.

EARS (MAKE 2)

Rnd 1: With light gray: start with a magic loop, 6sc in the loop. (6)
Rnd 2: 2sc in each stitch around. (12)
Rnd 3: *Sc1, 2sc in next*, repeat around. (18)
Rnd 4: *Sc2, 2sc in next*, repeat around. (24)
Rnds 5–10: Sc1 in each stitch around. (24)

Cut the yarn, but leave a long tail to attach the ears later; fold the ear flat and sew the bottom closed with the remaining yarn.

INNER EARS (MAKE 2)

Rnd 1: With white: start with a magic loop, 6sc in the loop. (6)
Rnd 2: *Sl st 1, ch2, 2dc in next stitch*, repeat from * to * 2 more times, sl st in first ch.

Cut yarn, leaving a long tail, and sew to the front of the ear.

BODY

Rnd 1: With light gray: ch18, 1dc in 3rd ch from hook, dc14, 3dc in last, continue along other side of chain, dc15, 3dc in last, sl st in first dc. (36)
Rnd 2: Ch2 (doesn't count as first stitch now and throughout), *dc17, 2dc in next*, repeat one more time, sl st in first dc. (38)
Rnd 3: Ch2, *dc18, 2dc in next*, repeat one more time, sl st in first dc. (40)
Rnd 4: Ch2, *dc19, 2dc in next*, repeat one more time, sl st in first dc. (42)
Rnd 5: Ch2, *dc20, 2dc in next*, repeat one more time, sl st in first dc. (44)
Rnd 6: Ch2, *dc21, 2dc in next*, repeat one more time, sl st in first dc. (46)

Rnd 7: Ch2, *dc22, 2dc in next*, repeat one more time, sl st in first dc. (48)

Rnd 8: Ch2, *dc23, 2dc in next*, repeat one more time, sl st in first dc. (50)

Rnd 9: Ch2, *dc24, 2dc in next*, repeat one more time, sl st in first dc. (52)

Rnd 10: Ch2, *dc25, 2dc in next*, repeat one more time, sl st in first dc. (54)

Rnd 11: Ch2, *dc26, 2dc in next*, repeat one more time, sl st in first dc. (56)

Rnd 12: Ch2, *dc27, 2dc in next*, repeat one more time, sl st in first dc. (58)

Rnd 13: Ch2, *dc28, 2dc in next*, repeat one more time, sl st in first dc. (60)

Rnd 14: Ch2, *dc29, 2dc in next*, repeat one more time, sl st in first dc. (62)

Rnd 15: Ch2, *dc30, 2dc in next*, repeat one more time, sl st in first dc. (64)

Rnd 16: Ch2, *dc31, 2dc in next*, repeat one more time, sl st in first dc. (66)

Rnd 17: Ch2, *dc32, 2dc in next*, repeat one more time, sl st in first dc. (68)

Rnd 18: Ch2, *dc33, 2dc in next*, repeat one more time, sl st in first dc. (70)

Cut a long tail to close the body later. Fold the body in line with the increases to make the belly straight.

LEGS (MAKE 2)

Rnd 1: With light gray: start with a magic loop, ch2 (doesn't count as first dc), dc12 in the loop, sl st in first dc. (12)

Rnd 2: Ch2, *dc1, 2dc in next*, repeat around, sl st in first dc. (18)

Rnds 3–6: Ch2, dc in each stitch around, sl st in first dc. (18)

Cut yarn and weave in ends.

ARMS (MAKE 2)

Rnd 1: With light gray: start with a magic loop, 6sc in the loop. (6)

Rnd 2: 2sc in each stitch around. (12)

Rnd 3: *Sc1, 2sc in next*, repeat around. (18)

Rnd 4: *Sc2, 2sc in next*, repeat around. (24)

Rnds 5–9: Sc1 in each stitch around. (24)

Rnd 10: *Sc2, sc2tog*, repeat around. (18)

Rnds 11–12: Sc1 in each stitch around. (18)

Rnd 13: Sl st 1, ch2 (doesn't count as first stitch now and throughout), dc in each stitch around, sl st in first dc. (18)

Rnd 14: Ch2, dc2tog, dc in each stitch around, sl st in first dc. (17)

At this point, stuff the hand. Take a small piece of the yarn and sew across the arm between rnds 12 and 13.

Rnd 15: Ch2, dc in each stitch around, sl st in first dc. (17)

Rnd 16: Ch2, dc2tog, dc in each stitch around, sl st in first dc. (16)

Rnd 17: Ch2, dc in each stitch around, sl st in first dc. (16)

Rnd 18: Ch2, dc2tog, dc in each stitch around, sl st in first dc. (15)

Rnd 19: Ch2, dc in each stitch around, sl st in first dc. (15)

Rnd 20: Ch2, dc2tog, dc in each stitch around, sl st in first dc. (14)

Rnd 21: Ch2, dc in each stitch around, sl st in first dc. (14)

Rnd 22: Ch2, dc2tog, dc in each stitch around, sl st in first dc. (13)

Cut a long tail to attach arms to body later.

PUTTING IT ALL TOGETHER

- Use pins to determine the placement of the ears. I attached them with a slight rounding, one corner in rnd 10 and the other corner in rnd 18. Sew the ears in place.
- Take the body and place both legs between the bottom two layers. With the remaining yarn from the body, sew across the seam with the legs in between. This way you close the bottom and assemble pieces at the same time.
- Sew an arm to each side of the body between rnds 1 and 3.
- Finally, sew rnd 21 of the head to rnd 1 of the body.

BABY KOALA

DIFFICULTY LEVEL: 2 of 5

SIZE: 7 in (18 cm) tall

MATERIALS

Yarn: DK #3 light weight yarn; shown in Scheepjes Stone Washed
- Light gray (Crystal Quartz 814): 142 yd (130 m)
- Black (Black Onyx 803): 54.5 yd (50 m)
- White (Moon Stone 801): 33 yd (30 m)

Crochet hook: US size D-3 (3 mm)

Other:
- Black safety eyes, 10 mm
- Fiberfill stuffing
- Needle and scissors

HEAD

Rnd 1: With light gray: start with a magic loop, 6sc in the loop. (6)
Rnd 2: 2sc in each stitch around. (12)
Rnd 3: *Sc1, 2sc in next*, repeat around. (18)
Rnd 4: *Sc2, 2sc in next*, repeat around. (24)
Rnd 5: *Sc3, 2sc in next*, repeat around. (30)
Rnd 6: *Sc4, 2sc in next*, repeat around. (36)
Rnds 7–12: Sc1 in each stitch around. (36)
Rnd 13: *Sc4, sc2tog*, repeat around. (30)
Rnd 14: *Sc3, sc2tog*, repeat around. (24)
Rnd 15: *Sc2, sc2tog*, repeat around. (18)

At this point, attach safety eyes between rnds 11 and 12, 9 stitches apart, and stuff the head.

Rnd 16: *Sc1, sc2tog*, repeat around. (12)
Rnd 17: *Sc2tog*, repeat around. (6)

Cut yarn, weave through remaining stitches, pull tight, and weave in ends.

EARS (MAKE 2)

Rnd 1: With light gray: start with a magic loop, 6sc in the loop. (6)
Rnd 2: 2sc in each stitch around. (12)
Rnd 3: *Sc1, 2sc in next*, repeat around. (18)
Rnds 4–6: Sc1 in each stitch around. (18)

Cut the yarn, but leave a long tail to attach the ears in the end; fold the ear flat and sew the bottom closed with the remaining yarn.

INNER EARS (MAKE 2)

Rnd 1: With white: start with a magic loop, 6sc in the loop. (6)
Rnd 2: *Sl st 1, ch2, 2dc in next stitch*, repeat from * to * 2 more times, sl st in first ch.

Cut yarn, leaving a long tail, and sew to the front of the ear.

NOSE

Rnd 1: With black: start with a magic loop, 6sc in the loop. (6)
Rnd 2: 2sc in first stitch, 2hdc in next stitch, 2dc in next stitch, 2hdc in next stitch, 2sc in each of the last 2 stitches. (12)

Cut a long tail and sew nose to head, centered between the eyes, from rnd 9 to rnd 14.

BODY

Rnd 1: With light gray: ch13, dc1 in 3rd ch from hook, dc9, 3dc in last, continue along the other side of the chains, dc10, 3dc in last, sl st in first dc. (26)
Rnd 2: Ch2 (doesn't count as first stitch now and throughout), *dc12, 2dc in next*, repeat one more time, sl st in first dc. (28)
Rnd 3: Ch2, *dc13, 2dc in next*, repeat one more time, sl st in first dc. (30)
Rnd 4: Ch2, *dc14, 2dc in next*, repeat one more time, sl st in first dc. (32)
Rnd 5: Ch2, *dc15, 2dc in next*, repeat one more time, sl st in first dc. (34)
Rnd 6: Ch2, *dc16, 2dc in next*, repeat one more time, sl st in first dc. (36)
Rnd 7: Ch2, *dc17, 2dc in next*, repeat one more time, sl st in first dc. (38)

Rnd 8: Ch2, *dc18, 2dc in next*, repeat one more time, sl st in first dc. (40)
Rnd 9: Ch2, *dc19, 2dc in next*, repeat one more time, sl st in first dc. (42)
Rnd 10: Ch2, *dc20, 2dc in next*, repeat one more time, sl st in first dc. (44)
Rnd 11: Ch2, *dc21, 2dc in next*, repeat one more time, sl st in first dc. (46)
Rnd 12: Ch2, *dc22, ch14, dc1 in 3rd ch from hook, dc1 in each of the remaining 11 chains, 2dc in next stitch of rnd 11*, repeat one more time, sl st in first dc.

Cut a long tail to close the body later.

ARMS (MAKE 2)

Rnd 1: With light gray: start with a magic loop, 6sc in the loop. (6)
Rnd 2: 2sc in each stitch around. (12)
Rnd 3: *Sc1, 2sc in next*, repeat around. (18)
Rnds 4–5: Sc1 in each stitch around. (18)
Rnd 6: *Sc1, sc2tog*, repeat around. (12)
Rnd 7: Sc1 in each stitch around. (12)
Rnd 8: Sl st 1, ch2 (doesn't count as first stitch now and throughout), dc in each stitch around, sl st in first dc. (12)
Rnd 9: Ch2, dc2tog, dc in each stitch around, sl st in first dc. (11)

At this point, stuff the hand. Take a small piece of light gray yarn and sew across the arm between rnds 7 and 8.

Rnd 10: Ch2, dc in each stitch around, sl st in first dc. (11)
Rnd 11: Ch2, dc2tog, dc in each stitch around, sl st in first dc. (10)
Rnd 12: Ch2, dc in each stitch around, sl st in first dc. (10)

Cut a long tail to attach arms to body later.

PUTTING IT ALL TOGETHER

- Use pins to determine the placement of the ears. I attached them with a slight rounding, one corner in rnd 7 and the other corner in rnd 12. Sew the ears in place.
- Fold the body in line with the increases to make the belly straight and sew closed with the remaining yarn. Tie a knot in the corners to form the feet.
- Sew an arm to each side of the body in rnds 1 and 2.
- Finally, sew rnd 14 of the head to rnd 1 of the body.

SANTA CLAUS

DIFFICULTY LEVEL: 3 of 5

SIZE: 12 in (30 cm) tall

MATERIALS

Yarn: DK #3 light weight yarn;
shown in Scheepjes Stone
Washed
- Red (Carnelian 823):
  142 yd (130 m)
- Light pink (Pink Quartz-
  ite 821): 76.5 yd (70 m)
- White (Moon Stone 801):
  65.5 yd (60 m)
- Black (Black Onyx 803):
  33 yd (30 m)

Crochet hook: US size D-3
(3 mm)

Other:
- Black safety eyes, 15 mm
- Fiberfill stuffing
- Needle and scissors

HEAD

Rnd 1: With light pink: ch23, 1sc in 2nd ch from
hook (this is your first stitch), sc20, 4sc in last,
continue along the other side of the chains,
sc20, 3sc in last. (48)

Rnds 2–17: Sc in each stitch around. (48)

Attach the safety eyes between rnds 10 and 11,
with 13 stitches in between.

Rnd 18: *Sc6, sc2tog*, repeat around. (42)
Rnd 19: *Sc5, sc2tog*, repeat around. (36)
Rnd 20: *Sc4, sc2tog*, repeat around. (30)
Rnd 21: *Sc3, sc2tog*, repeat around. (24)
Rnd 22: *Sc2, sc2tog*, repeat around. (18)

Stuff the head.

Rnd 23: *Sc1, sc2tog*, repeat around. (12)

Cut a long tail, close the seam, and weave in
ends.

HAT

Rnd 1: With white: start with a magic loop, 6sc in
the loop. (6)
Rnd 2: 2sc in each stitch around. (12)
Rnd 3: *Sc1, 2sc in next*, repeat around. (18)
Rnd 4: *Sc2, 2sc in next*, repeat around. (24)
Rnds 5–7: Sc in each stitch around. (24)

Rnd 8: *Sc2, sc2tog*, repeat around. (18)
Rnd 9: *Sc1, sc2tog*, repeat around. (12)

Stuff the pom-pom.

Rnd 10: Sc2tog in each stitch around. (6)

Cut the white yarn.

Rnd 11: With red: 1 sl st, ch2 (doesn't count as first stitch for the entire pattern), dc in each stitch around, sl st in first dc. (6)
Rnd 12: Ch2, *dc1, 2dc in next*, repeat around, sl st in first dc. (9)
Rnd 13: Ch2, *dc2, 2dc in next*, repeat around, sl st in first dc. (12)
Rnd 14: Ch2, *dc3, 2dc in next*, repeat around, sl st in first dc. (15)
Rnd 15: Ch2, *dc4, 2dc in next*, repeat around, sl st in first dc. (18)
Rnd 16: Ch2, *dc5, 2dc in next*, repeat around, sl st in first dc. (21)
Rnd 17: Ch2, *dc6, 2dc in next*, repeat around, sl st in first dc. (24)
Rnd 18: Ch2, *dc7, 2dc in next*, repeat around, sl st in first dc. (27)
Rnd 19: Ch2, *dc8, 2dc in next*, repeat around, sl st in first dc. (30)
Rnd 20: Ch2, *dc9, 2dc in next*, repeat around, sl st in first dc. (33)
Rnd 21: Ch2, *dc10, 2dc in next*, repeat around, sl st in first dc. (36)
Rnd 22: Ch2, *dc11, 2dc in next*, repeat around, sl st in first dc. (39)
Rnd 23: Ch2, *dc12, 2dc in next*, repeat around, sl st in first dc. (42)
Rnd 24: Ch2, *dc13, 2dc in next*, repeat around, sl st in first dc. (45)
Rnd 25: Ch2, *dc14, 2dc in next*, repeat around, sl st in first dc. (48)
Rnd 26: With white (cut the red yarn), ch2, dc in each stitch around, sl st in first dc. (48)
Rnds 27–29: Ch2, dc in each stitch around, sl st in first dc. (48)

Cut a long tail to attach hat later and fold the brim.

BEARD

Rnd 1: With white: ch9, 1dc in 3rd ch from hook (first ch2 doesn't count as first dc now and throughout), *dc4tog in next stitch, dc1*, repeat from * to * to end. (7)
Rnd 2: Ch2, turn, 3dc in same as ch2, *dc4tog in next stitch, dc1*, repeat from * to * one more time, dc4tog in next stitch, 3dc in last. (11)
Rnd 3: Ch2, turn, 3dc in same as ch2, *dc4tog in next stitch, dc1*, repeat from * to * 3 more times, dc4tog in next stitch, 3dc in last. (15)
Rnd 4: Ch2, turn, 3dc in same as ch2, *dc4tog in next stitch, dc1*, repeat from * to * 5 more times, dc4tog in next stitch, 3dc in last. (19)
Rnd 5: Ch2, turn, 3dc in same as ch2, *dc4tog in next stitch, dc1*, repeat from * to * 7 more times, dc4tog in next stitch, 3dc in last. (23)

Cut a long tail to attach beard later.

MUSTACHE

Rnd 1: With white: start with a magic loop, ch4, {in the loop: trl, ch3, sl st in first ch of ch3, trl, dc1, hdc1, sc1, sl st 1, sc1, hdc1, dc1, trl, ch3, sl st in first ch of ch3, trl, ch4, sl st 1}. Pull the yarn tight and wind the yarn around the center twice.

Cut a long tail to attach the mustache later.

BODY

Rnd 1: With red: ch18, 1dc in 3rd ch from hook, dc14, 3dc in last, continue along the other side of the chains, dc15, 3dc in last, sl st in first dc. (36)

Rnd 2: Ch2 (doesn't count as first stitch now and throughout), *dc17, 2dc in next*, repeat one more time, sl st in first dc. (38)

Rnd 3: Ch2, *dc18, 2dc in next*, repeat one more time, sl st in first dc. (40)

Rnd 4: Ch2, *dc19, 2dc in next*, repeat one more time, sl st in first dc. (42)

Rnd 5: Ch2, *dc20, 2dc in next*, repeat one more time, sl st in first dc. (44)

Rnd 6: Ch2, *dc21, 2dc in next*, repeat one more time, sl st in first dc. (46)

Rnd 7: Ch2, *dc22, 2dc in next*, repeat one more time, sl st in first dc. (48)

Rnd 8: Ch2, *dc23, 2dc in next*, repeat one more time, sl st in first dc. (50)

Rnd 9: Ch2, *dc24, 2dc in next*, repeat one more time, sl st in first dc. (52)

Rnd 10: With black: *dc25, 2dc in next*, repeat one more time, sl st in first dc. (54)

You can cut the black yarn.

Rnd 11: With red: ch2, *dc26, 2dc in next*, repeat one more time, sl st in first dc. (56)

Rnd 12: Ch2, *dc27, 2dc in next*, repeat one more time, sl st in first dc. (58)

Rnd 13: Ch2, *dc28, 2dc in next*, repeat one more time, sl st in first dc. (60)

Rnd 14: Ch2, *dc29, 2dc in next*, repeat one more time, sl st in first dc. (62)

Rnd 15: Ch2, *dc30, 2dc in next*, repeat one more time, sl st in first dc. (64)

Cut a long tail to close the body later. Fold the body in line with the increases to make the belly straight.

ARMS (MAKE 2)

Rnd 1: With light pink: start with a magic loop, 6sc in the loop. (6)

Rnd 2: 2sc in each stitch around. (12)

Rnd 3: *Sc1, 2sc in next*, repeat around. (18)

Rnd 4: *Sc2, 2sc in next*, repeat around. (24)

Rnds 5–9: Sc in each stitch around. (24)

Rnd 10: *Sc2, sc2tog*, repeat around. (18)

Rnds 11–12: Sc in each stitch around. (18)

Rnd 13: With white (cut the light pink yarn, but leave a long tail to sew the hand shut after rnd 14): sl st 1, ch2 (doesn't count as first stitch now and throughout), dc in each stitch around, sl st in first dc. (18)

Rnd 14: With red (cut the white yarn): in back loops only, ch2, dc2tog, dc in each stitch around, sl st in first dc. (17)

At this point, stuff the hand; take the remaining light pink yarn and sew across the arm between rnds 12 and 13.

Rnd 15: Ch2, dc in each stitch around, sl st in first dc. (17)

Rnd 16: Ch2, dc2tog, dc in each stitch around, sl st in first dc. (16)

Rnd 17: Ch2, dc in each stitch around, sl st in first dc. (16)

Rnd 18: Ch2, dc2tog, dc in each stitch around, sl st in first dc. (15)

Rnd 19: Ch2, dc in each stitch around, sl st in first dc. (15)

Rnd 20: Ch2, dc2tog, dc in each stitch around, sl st in first dc. (14)

Rnd 21: Ch2, dc in each stitch around, sl st in first dc. (14)

Rnd 22: Ch2, dc2tog, dc in each stitch around, sl st in first dc. (13)

Cut a long tail to attach arms later.

LEGS (MAKE 2)

Rnd 1: With black: start with a magic loop, ch2 (doesn't count as first stitch now and through-out), 12dc in the loop, sl st in first dc. (12)

Rnd 2: Ch2, *dc1, 2dc in next*, repeat around, sl st in first dc. (18)

Rnds 3–4: Ch2, dc in each stitch around, sl st in first dc. (18)

Rnd 5: With white (cut the black yarn): ch2, dc in each stitch around, sl st in first dc. (18)

Rnd 6: With red (cut the white yarn): in back loops ch2, dc in each stitch around, sl st in first dc. (18)

Rnds 7–10: Ch2, dc in each stitch around, sl st in first dc. (18)

Cut the yarn and weave in ends.

PUTTING IT ALL TOGETHER

- Put the hat on the head, just above the eyes, and sew in place.
- Sew the beard and mustache to the face.
- Take the body and place both legs between the bottom two layers. With the remaining yarn from the body, sew across the seam with legs in between. This way you close the bottom and assemble pieces at the same time.
- Sew an arm to each side of the body between rnds 1 and 3.
- Take the head and sew rnd 19 of the head to rnd 1 of the body.

REINDEER

DIFFICULTY LEVEL: 2 of 5

SIZE: 12 in (30 cm) tall

MATERIALS

Yarn: DK #3 light weight yarn;
shown in Scheepjes Stone
Washed
- Light brown (Boulder
  Opal 804): 142 yd (130 m)
- Dark brown (Brown Ag-
  ate 822): 109.5 yd (100 m)

Crochet hook: US size D-3
(3 mm)

Other:
- Black and brown safety
  eyes, 15 mm
- Fiberfill stuffing
- Needle and scissors

HEAD

Rnd 1: With light brown: start with a magic loop,
6sc in the loop. (6)

Rnd 2: 2sc in each stitch around. (12)

Rnd 3: *Sc1, 2sc in next*, repeat around. (18)

Rnd 4: *Sc2, 2sc in next*, repeat around. (24)

Rnd 5: *Sc3, 2sc in next*, repeat around. (30)

Rnd 6: *Sc4, 2sc in next*, repeat around. (36)

Rnd 7: *Sc5, 2sc in next*, repeat around. (42)

Rnd 8: *Sc6, 2sc in next*, repeat around. (48)

Rnds 9–20: Sc1 in each stitch around. (48)

Rnd 21: *Sc7, 2sc in next*, repeat around. (54)

Rnd 22: Sc1 in each stitch around. (54)

Rnd 23: *Sc8, 2sc in next*, repeat around. (60)

Rnd 24: Sc1 in each stitch around. (60)

Rnd 25: *Sc9, 2sc in next*, repeat around. (66)

Rnds 26–28: Sc1 in each stitch around. (66)

Rnd 29: *Sc9, sc2tog*, repeat around. (60)

Rnd 30: *Sc8, sc2tog*, repeat around. (54)

Rnd 31: *Sc7, sc2tog*, repeat around. (48)

Rnd 32: *Sc6, sc2tog*, repeat around. (42)

Rnd 33: *Sc5, sc2tog*, repeat around. (36)

Rnd 34: *Sc4, sc2tog*, repeat around. (30)

Rnd 35: *Sc3, sc2tog*, repeat around. (24)

Rnd 36: *Sc2, sc2tog*, repeat around. (18)

Attach the eyes between rnds 20 and 21, 12
stitches apart, and stuff the head.

Rnd 37: *Sc1, sc2tog*, repeat around. (12)
Rnd 38: *Sc2tog*, repeat around. (6)

Cut yarn, weave through remaining stitches, pull tight, and weave in ends.

NOSE

Rnd 1: With dark brown: start with a magic loop, 6sc in the loop. (6)
Rnd 2: *Sc1, 3sc in next*, repeat around. (12)
Rnd 3: Sc2, 3sc in next, sc3, 3sc in next, sc4, 3sc in next. (18)
Rnd 4: Sc4, 3sc in next, sc5, 3sc in next, sc6, sl st in last sc. (22)

Cut a long tail and sew nose to head, centered between the eyes, from rnds 22 to 30.

LARGE ANTLER (MAKE 2)

Rnd 1: With dark brown: start with a magic loop, 6sc in the loop. (6)
Rnd 2: 2sc in each stitch around. (12)
Rnds 3–15: Sc1 in each stitch around. (12)

Stuff the antler evenly. Cut the yarn, but leave a long tail to attach the antlers to each side of the head from rnds 5 to 8.

SMALLER ANTLER (MAKE 2)

Rnd 1: With dark brown: start with a magic loop, 8sc in the loop. (8)
Rnds 2–6: Sc1 in each stitch around. (8)

Stuff the antler evenly. Cut the yarn, but leave a long tail to attach the smaller antlers to the inside of the large antler on each side, between rnds 6 and 9. You can add an extra stitch a few rounds higher to make it bend toward the large antler.

EARS (MAKE 2)

Rnd 1: With light brown: start with a magic loop, 6sc in the loop. (6) Don't close this rnd, but continue working flat.
Row 2: Turn, ch1 (doesn't count as first stitch for entire ear), sc1, 2dc in each of the next 4 stitches, sc1 in last. (10)
Row 3: Turn, ch1, 2sc in first sc, 1dc in each of the next 8 stitches, 2sc in last. (12)

Cut a long tail, sew ears closed on the bottom (these are the first and last sc of the rnds), and attach to both sides of the head in rnd 10 next to the antler.

BODY

Rnd 1: With light brown: ch18, 1dc in 3rd ch from hook, dc14, 3dc in last, continue along other side of chain, dc15, 3dc in last, sl st in first dc. (36)
Rnd 2: Ch2 (doesn't count as first stitch now and throughout), *dc17, 2dc in next*, repeat one more time, sl st in first dc. (38)
Rnd 3: Ch2, *dc18, 2dc in next*, repeat one more time, sl st in first dc. (40)
Rnd 4: Ch2, *dc19, 2dc in next*, repeat one more time, sl st in first dc. (42)
Rnd 5: Ch2, *dc20, 2dc in next*, repeat one more time, sl st in first dc. (44)
Rnd 6: Ch2, *dc21, 2dc in next*, repeat one more time, sl st in first dc. (46)
Rnd 7: Ch2, *dc22, 2dc in next*, repeat one more time, sl st in first dc. (48)
Rnd 8: Ch2, *dc23, 2dc in next*, repeat one more time, sl st in first dc. (50)
Rnd 9: Ch2, *dc24, 2dc in next*, repeat one more time, sl st in first dc. (52)
Rnd 10: Ch2, *dc25, 2dc in next*, repeat one more time, sl st in first dc. (54)

Rnd 11: Ch2, *dc26, 2dc in next*, repeat one more time, sl st in first dc. (56)

Rnd 12: Ch2, *dc27, 2dc in next*, repeat one more time, sl st in first dc. (58)

Rnd 13: Ch2, *dc28, 2dc in next*, repeat one more time, sl st in first dc. (60)

Rnd 14: Ch2, *dc29, 2dc in next*, repeat one more time, sl st in first dc. (62)

Rnd 15: Ch2, *dc30, 2dc in next*, repeat one more time, sl st in first dc. (64)

Rnd 16: Ch2, *dc31, 2dc in next*, repeat one more time, sl st in first dc. (66)

Rnd 17: Ch2, *dc32, 2dc in next*, repeat one more time, sl st in first dc. (68)

Rnd 18: Ch2, *dc33, 2dc in next*, repeat one more time, sl st in first dc. (70)

Cut a long tail to close the body later. Fold the body in line with the increases to make the belly straight.

LEGS (MAKE 2)

Rnd 1: With dark brown: start with a magic loop, ch2 (doesn't count as first dc), 12dc in the loop, sl st in first dc. (12)

Rnd 2: Ch2, *dc1, 2dc in next*, repeat around, sl st in first dc. (18)

Rnd 3: Ch2, dc in each stitch around, sl st in first dc. (18)

Rnds 4–8: With light brown: ch2, dc in each stitch around, sl st in first dc. (18)

Cut yarn and weave in ends.

ARMS (MAKE 2)

Rnd 1: With dark brown: start with a magic loop, 6sc in the loop. (6)

Rnd 2: 2sc in each stitch around. (12)

Rnd 3: *Sc1, 2sc in next*, repeat around. (18)

Rnd 4: *Sc2, 2sc in next*, repeat around. (24)

Rnds 5–9: Sc in each stitch around. (24)

Rnd 10: *Sc2, sc2tog*, repeat around. (18)

Rnds 11–12: Sc in each stitch around. (18)

Cut a long tail; you'll use it after rnd 14.

Rnd 13: With light brown: sl st 1, ch2 (doesn't count as first stitch now and throughout), dc in each stitch around, sl st in first dc. (18)

Rnd 14: Ch2, dc2tog, dc in each stitch around, sl st in first dc. (17)

At this point, stuff the hand. Take the remaining dark brown yarn and sew across the arm between rnds 12 and 13.

Rnd 15: Ch2, dc in each stitch around, sl st in first dc. (17)

Rnd 16: Ch2, dc2tog, dc in each stitch around, sl st in first dc. (16)

Rnd 17: Ch2, dc in each stitch around, sl st in first dc. (16)

Rnd 18: Ch2, dc2tog, dc in each stitch around, sl st in first dc. (15)

Rnd 19: Ch2, dc in each stitch around, sl st in first dc. (15)

Rnd 20: Ch2, dc2tog, dc in each stitch around, sl st in first dc. (14)

Rnd 21: Ch2, dc in each stitch around, sl st in first dc. (14)

Cut a long tail to attach arms to body later.

ARMS (MAKE 2)

Rnd 1: With dark brown: start with a magic loop, 6sc in the loop. (6)

Rnd 2: 2sc in each stitch around. (12)

Rnd 3: *Sc1, 2sc in next*, repeat around. (18)

Rnds 4–5: Sc in each stitch around. (18)

Rnd 6: *Sc1, sc2tog*, repeat around. (12)

Rnd 7: Sc in each stitch around. (12)

Cut a long tail; you'll use it after rnd 9.

Rnd 8: With light brown, sl st 1, ch2 (doesn't count as first stitch now and throughout), dc in each stitch around, sl st in first dc. (12)

Rnd 9: Ch2, dc2tog, dc in each stitch around, sl st in first dc. (11)

At this point, stuff the hand. Take the remaining light brown yarn and sew across the arm between rnds 7 and 8.

Rnd 10: Ch2, dc in each stitch around, sl st in first dc. (11)

Rnd 11: Ch2, dc2tog, dc in each stitch around, sl st in first dc. (10)

Rnd 12: Ch2, dc in each stitch around, sl st in first dc. (10)

Cut a long tail to attach arms to body later.

PUTTING IT ALL TOGETHER

- Fold the body in line with the increases to make the belly straight and sew closed with the remaining yarn. Tie a knot in the corners to form the feet.
- Sew an arm to each side of the body between rnds 1 and 2.
- Sew rnd 16 of the head to rnd 1 of the body.

GIRAFFE

DIFFICULTY LEVEL: 4 of 5

SIZE: 13.5 in (35 cm) tall

MATERIALS

Yarn: DK #3 light weight yarn;
shown in Scheepjes Stone
Washed
- Brown (Brown Agate
  822): 142.5 yd (130 m)
- Yellow (Yellow Jasper
  809): 142.5 yd (130 m)

Crochet hook: US size D-3
(3 mm)

Other:
- Black and brown safety
  eyes, 15 mm
- Fiberfill stuffing
- Needle and scissors

EARS (MAKE 2)

Rnd 1: With yellow: start with a magic ring, 6sc in
the ring. (6)
Rnd 2: Sc1 in each stitch around. (6)
Rnd 3: 2sc in each stitch around. (12)
Rnds 4–5: Sc1 in each stitch around. (12)
Rnd 6: *Sc1, 2sc in next*, repeat around. (18)
Rnd 7: Sc1 in each stitch around. (18)

For first ear, cut yarn and weave in ends. For second ear, don't cut yarn and continue with head instructions.

HEAD

Rnd 1: Continue with the yellow yarn from the
second ear, ch9, take first ear, sc1 in each of
the 18 stitches of first ear, sc1 in each of the
9 chains you just made, sc1 in each of the 18
stitches of second ear. (54)
Rnd 2: Sc1 in each stitch around. (54)
Rnd 3: Sc18, sc2tog, sc25, sc2tog, sc7. (52)
Rnd 4: Sc1 in each stitch around. (52)
Rnd 5: Sc18, sc2tog, sc24, sc2tog, sc6. (50)
Rnd 6: Sc1 in each stitch around. (50)
Rnd 7: Sc18, sc2tog, sc23, sc2tog, sc5. (48)
Rnd 8: Sc1 in each stitch around. (48)
Rnd 9: Sc18, sc2tog, sc22, sc2tog, sc4. (46)
Rnd 10: Sc1 in each stitch around. (46)
Rnd 11: Sc18, sc2tog, sc21, sc2tog, sc3. (44)

Rnd 12: Sc1 in each stitch around. (44)
Rnd 13: Sc18, sc2tog, sc20, sc2tog, sc2. (42)
Rnd 14: Sc1 in each stitch around. (42)
Rnd 15: Sc18, sc2tog, sc19, sc2tog, sc1. (40)
Rnd 16: Sc1 in each stitch around. (40)
Rnd 17: Sc18, sc2tog, sc18, sc2tog. (38)
Rnd 18: Sc1 in each stitch around. (38)
Rnd 19: Sc18, sc2tog, sc16, sc2tog. (36)
Rnd 20: Sc1 in each stitch around. (36)
Rnds 21–24: With brown, sc1 in each stitch around. (36)

Cut the yellow yarn.

Rnd 25: *Sc4, sc2tog*, repeat around. (30)
Rnd 26: *Sc3, sc2tog*, repeat around. (24)
Rnd 27: *Sc2, sc2tog*, repeat around. (18)

Attach the 15 mm safety eyes between rnds 12 and 13 of the head, and stuff the head.

Rnd 28: *Sc1, sc2tog*, repeat around. (12)

Fold seam flat and sew front and back of head together; weave in ends.

BODY

Rnd 1: With brown, ch18, 1dc in 3rd ch from hook, dc4, with yellow: dc2, with brown: dc8, 3dc in last, continue along other side of chains, dc5, with yellow: dc2, with brown: dc8, 3dc in last, sl st in first dc. (36)
Rnd 2: With brown: ch2 (doesn't count as first stitch now and throughout), *with brown: dc5, with yellow: dc2, with brown: dc10, 2dc in next*, repeat one more time, sl st in first dc. (38)
Rnd 3: With brown: ch2, *with brown: dc4, with yellow: dc2, with brown: dc2, with yellow: dc2, with brown: dc8, 2dc in next*, repeat one more time, sl st in first dc. (40)

Rnd 4: With brown: ch2, *with brown: dc3, with yellow: dc2, with brown: dc5, with yellow: dc2, with brown: dc6, with yellow: dc1, 2dc in next*, repeat one more time, sl st in first dc. (42)
Rnd 5: With yellow: ch2, *with yellow: dc4, with brown: dc8, with yellow: dc8, 2dc in next*, repeat one more time, sl st in first dc. (44)
Rnd 6: With brown: ch2, *with brown: dc3, with yellow: dc2, with brown: dc8, with yellow: dc1, with brown: dc7, 2dc in next*, repeat one more time, sl st in first dc. (46)
Rnd 7: With brown: ch2, *with brown: dc4, with yellow: dc2, with brown: dc6, with yellow: dc2, with brown: dc8, 2dc in next*, repeat one more time, sl st in first dc. (48)
Rnd 8: With brown: ch2, *with brown: dc5, with yellow: dc2, with brown: dc5, with yellow: dc2, with brown: dc9, 2dc in next*, repeat one more time, sl st in first dc. (50)
Rnd 9: With brown: ch2, *with brown: dc7, with yellow: dc6, with brown: dc11, 2dc in next*, repeat one more time, sl st in first dc. (52)
Rnd 10: With brown: ch2, *with brown: dc8, with yellow: dc2, with brown: dc2, with yellow: dc2, with brown: dc11, with yellow: 2dc in next*, repeat one more time, sl st in first dc. (54)
Rnd 11: With brown: ch2, *with brown: dc7, with yellow: dc2, with brown: dc5, with yellow: dc2, with brown: dc7, with yellow: dc3, with brown: 2dc in next*, repeat one more time, sl st in first dc. (56)
Rnd 12: With brown: ch2, *with brown: dc5, with yellow: dc3, with brown: dc8, with yellow: dc3, with brown: dc3, with yellow: dc2, with brown: dc3, 2dc in next*, repeat one more time, sl st in first dc. (58)
Rnd 13: With yellow: ch2, *with yellow: dc6, with brown: dc12, with yellow: dc5, with brown: dc5, 2dc in next*, repeat one more time, sl st in first dc. (60)

Rnd 14: With brown: ch2, *with brown: dc5, with yellow: dc2, with brown: dc12, with yellow: dc3, with brown: dc7, 2dc in next*, repeat one more time, sl st in first dc. (62)

Rnd 15: With brown: ch2, *with brown: dc6, with yellow: dc2, with brown: dc10, with yellow: dc2, with brown: dc2, with yellow: dc2, with brown: dc6, 2dc in next*, repeat one more time, sl st in first dc. (64)

Rnd 16: With brown: ch2, *with brown: dc8, with yellow: dc2, with brown: dc7, with yellow: dc2, with brown: dc4, with yellow: dc2, with brown: dc6, 2dc in next*, repeat one more time, sl st in first dc. (66)

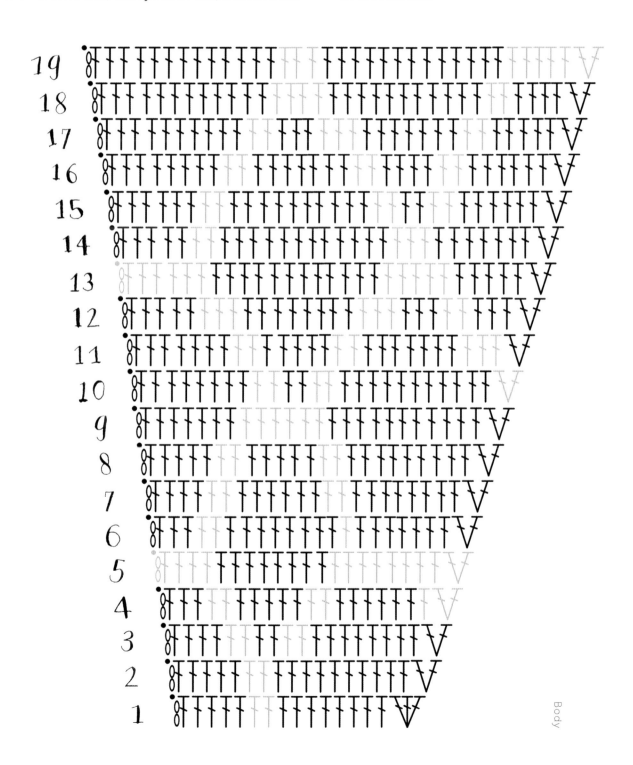

Rnd 17: With brown: ch2, *with brown: dc10, with yellow: dc2, with brown: dc3, with yellow: dc3, with brown: dc7, with yellow: dc2, with brown: dc5, 2dc in next*, repeat one more time, sl st in first dc. (68)

Rnd 18: With brown: ch2, *with brown: dc12, with yellow: dc4, with brown: dc11, with yellow: dc2, with brown: dc4, 2dc in next*, repeat one more time, sl st in first dc. (70)

Rnd 19: With brown: ch2, *with brown: dc13, with yellow: dc3, with brown: dc13, with yellow: dc5, 2dc in next*, repeat one more time, sl st in first dc. (72)

Cut the yellow yarn and weave in ends. Cut a long tail of the brown yarn to close the body later. Fold the body in line with the increases to make the belly straight.

LEGS (MAKE 2)

Rnd 1: With brown, start with a magic ring, 6sc in the ring. (6)

Rnd 2: 2sc in each stitch around. (12)

Rnd 3: *Sc1, 2sc in next*, repeat around. (18)

Rnd 4: In back loops only, sc1 in each stitch around. (18)

Rnds 5–9: Sc1 in each stitch around. (18)

Cut a long brown tail to use after rnd 11.

Rnd 10: With yellow, sl st 1, ch2 (doesn't count as first stitch now and throughout), dc1 in each stitch around, sl st in first dc. (18)

Rnd 11: Ch2, dc2tog, dc1 in each stitch around, sl st in first dc. (17)

Stuff and sew across leg with the brown yarn end between rnds 9 and 10.

Rnd 12: Ch2, dc1 in each stitch around, sl st in first dc. (17)

Rnd 13: Ch2, dc2tog, dc1 in each stitch around, sl st in first dc. (16)

Rnd 14: Ch2, dc1 in each stitch around, sl st in first dc. (16)

Rnd 15: Ch2, dc2tog, dc1 in each stitch around, sl st in first dc. (15)

Cut yarn and weave in ends.

ARMS (MAKE 2)

Rnd 1: With brown: start with a magic ring, 6sc in the ring. (6)

Rnd 2: 2sc in each stitch around. (12)

Rnd 3: *Sc1, 2sc in next*, repeat around. (18)

Rnd 4: In back loops only, sc1 in each stitch around. (18)

Rnds 5–9: Sc1 in each stitch around. (18)

Cut a long brown tail to use after rnd 11.

Rnd 10: With yellow, sl st 1, ch2, dc1 in each stitch around, sl st in first dc. (18)

Rnd 11: Ch2, dc2tog, dc1 in each stitch around, sl st in first dc. (17)

Stuff and sew across arm with the brown yarn end between rnds 9 and 10.

Rnd 12: Ch2, dc1 in each stitch around, sl st in first dc. (17)

Rnd 13: Ch2, dc2tog, dc1 in each stitch around, sl st in first dc. (16)

Rnd 14: Ch2, dc1 in each stitch around, sl st in first dc. (16)

Rnd 15: Ch2, dc2tog, dc1 in each stitch around, sl st in first dc. (15)

Rnd 16: Ch2, dc1 in each stitch around, sl st in first dc. (15)

Rnd 17: Ch2, dc2tog, dc1 in each stitch around, sl st in first dc. (14)

Rnd 18: Ch2, dc1 in each stitch around, sl st in first dc. (14)

Rnd 19: Ch2, dc2tog, dc1 in each stitch around, sl st in first dc. (13)

Cut a long tail to attach arms to body later.

HORNS (MAKE 2)

Rnd 1: With brown: start with a magic ring, 6sc in the ring. (6)
Rnd 2: 2sc in each stitch around. (12)
Rnd 3: *Sc1, 2sc in next* repeat around. (18)
Rnd 4: *Sc1, sc2tog* repeat around. (12)

Rnd 5: *Sc1, sc2tog* repeat around. (8)

Stuff the brown part of the horn.

Rnd 6: Change to yellow, sc1 in each stitch around. (8)

Cut the brown yarn.

Rnds 7–9: Sc1 in each stitch around. (8)

Cut a long tail to sew the horn to the head.

PUTTING IT ALL TOGETHER

- Sew horns to the head on the inside of both ears, slightly to the front.
- Take the body and place both legs between the bottom two layers. With the remaining yarn from the body, sew across the seam with the legs in between. This way you close the bottom and assemble pieces at the same time.
- Sew an arm to each side of the body between rnds 1 and 3.
- Finally, sew rnd 21 of the head to rnd 1 of the body.

BABY GIRAFFE

DIFFICULTY LEVEL: 4 of 5

SIZE: 7 in (18 cm) tall

MATERIALS

Yarn: DK #3 light weight yarn; shown in Scheepjes Stone Washed
- Brown (Brown Agate 822): 76.5 yd (70 m)
- Yellow (Yellow Jasper 809): 76.5 yd (70 m)

Crochet hook: US size D-3 (3 mm)

Other:
- Black and brown safety eyes, 12 mm
- Fiberfill stuffing
- Needle and scissors

EARS (MAKE 2)

Rnd 1: With yellow: start with a magic ring, 6sc in the ring. (6)
Rnd 2: Sc1 in each stitch around. (6)
Rnd 3: 2sc in each stitch around. (12)
Rnds 4 and 5: Sc1 in each stitch around. (12)

For first ear, cut yarn and weave in ends. For second ear, don't cut yarn and continue with head instructions.

HEAD

Rnd 1: Continue with the yellow yarn that's already on your hook: ch6, take first ear, sc1 in each of the 12 stitches of first ear, sc1 in each of the 6 chains you just made, continue in second ear, sc1 in each of the 12 stitches of second ear, sc1 in the other side of each of the 6 chains you just made. (36)
Rnd 2: Sc12, sc2tog, sc16, sc2tog, sc4. (34)
Rnd 3: Sc1 in each stitch around. (34)
Rnd 4: Sc12, sc2tog, sc15, sc2tog, sc3. (32)
Rnd 5: Sc1 in each stitch around. (32)
Rnd 6: Sc12, sc2tog, sc14, sc2tog, sc2. (30)
Rnd 7: Sc1 in each stitch around. (30)
Rnd 8: Sc12, sc2tog, sc13, sc2tog, sc1. (28)
Rnd 9: Sc1 in each stitch around. (28)
Rnd 10: Sc12, sc2tog, sc12, sc2tog. (26)
Rnd 11: Sc1 in each stitch around. (26)

Rnd 12: Sc12, change to brown (you can cut the yellow yarn), sc2tog, sc10, sc2tog. (24)
Rnd 13: Sc1 in each stitch around. (24)
Rnd 14: *Sc2, sc2tog*, repeat around. (18)

Attach safety eyes between rnds 6 and 7 of the head (ears not included). Stuff the head and ears.

Rnd 15: *Sc1, sc2tog*, repeat around. (12)
Rnd 16: *Sc2tog*, repeat around. (6)

Cut a long tail, and sew the seam of the mouth closed.

HORNS (MAKE 2)

Rnd 1: With brown: start with a magic ring, 6sc in the ring. (6)
Rnd 2: 2sc in each stitch around. (12)
Rnd 3: Sc2tog in each stitch around. (6)
Rnd 4: Change to yellow, sc1 in each stitch around. (6)

Cut the brown yarn.

Rnd 5: Sc1 in each stitch around. (6)

Cut a long tail, sew horn to head next to the ear and slightly in front of it, next to the center on each side.

ARMS (MAKE 2)

Rnd 1: With brown: start with a magic loop, 6sc in the loop. (6)
Rnd 2: 2sc in each stitch around. (12)
Rnd 3: In back loops only, sc1 in each stitch around. (12)
Rnds 4–6: Sc1 in each stitch around. (12)

Cut a long tail; you'll use it after rnd 8.

Rnd 7: With yellow: sl st 1, ch2 (doesn't count as first stitch now and throughout), dc1 in each stitch around, sl st in first dc. (12)
Rnd 8: Ch2, dc2tog, dc1 in each stitch around, sl st in first dc. (11)

At this point, stuff the hand. Take the remaining brown yarn and sew across the arm between rnds 6 and 7.

Rnd 9: Ch2, dc1 in each stitch around, sl st in first dc. (11)
Rnd 10: Ch2, dc2tog, dc1 in each stitch around, sl st in first dc. (10)
Rnd 11: Ch2, dc1 in each stitch around, sl st in first dc. (10)
Rnd 12: Ch2, dc2tog, dc1 in each stitch around, sl st in first dc. (9)

Cut a long tail to attach arms to body later.

BODY

Rnd 1: With brown: ch13, 1dc in 3rd ch from hook, dc3, with yellow: dc2, with brown: dc4, 3dc in last, continue along other side of chains, with brown: dc4, with yellow: dc2, with brown: dc4, 3dc in last, sl st in first dc. (26)
Rnd 2: With brown: ch2 (doesn't count as first stitch now and throughout), *with brown: dc4, with yellow: dc3, with brown: dc5, 2dc in next*, repeat one more time, sl st in first dc. (28)
Rnd 3: With brown: ch2, *with brown: dc3, with yellow: dc2, with brown: dc2, with yellow: dc2, with brown: dc4, 2dc in next*, repeat one more time, sl st in first dc. (30)
Rnd 4: With yellow: ch2, *with yellow: dc4, with brown: dc4, with yellow: dc4, with brown: dc2, 2dc in next*, repeat one more time, sl st in first dc. (32)
Rnd 5: With brown: ch2, *with brown: dc2, with yellow: dc2, with brown: dc7, with yellow: dc4, 2dc in next*, repeat one more time, sl st in first dc. (34)

Rnd 6: With brown: ch2, *with brown: dc3, with yellow: dc2, with brown: dc5, with yellow: dc2, with brown: dc4, 2dc in next*, repeat one more time, sl st in first dc. (36)

Rnd 7: With brown: ch2, *with brown: dc4, with yellow: dc2, with brown: dc2, with yellow: dc3, with brown: dc6, with yellow: 2dc in next*, repeat one more time, sl st in first dc. (38)

Rnd 8: With brown: ch2, *with brown: dc6, with yellow: dc3, with brown: dc7, with yellow: dc2, with brown: 2dc in next*, repeat one more time, sl st in first dc. (40)

Rnd 9: With brown: ch2, *with brown: dc5, with yellow: dc2, with brown: dc2, with yellow: dc2, with brown: dc5, with yellow: dc2, with brown: dc1, 2dc in next*, repeat one more time, sl st in first dc. (42)

Rnd 10: With brown: ch2, *with brown: dc4, with yellow: dc2, with brown: dc4, with yellow: dc3, with brown: dc2, with yellow: dc2, with brown: dc3, 2dc in next*, repeat one more time, sl st in first dc. (44)

Rnd 11: With brown: ch2, *with brown: dc2, with yellow: dc3, with brown: dc8, with yellow: dc3, with brown: dc5, 2dc in next*, repeat one more time, sl st in first dc. (46)

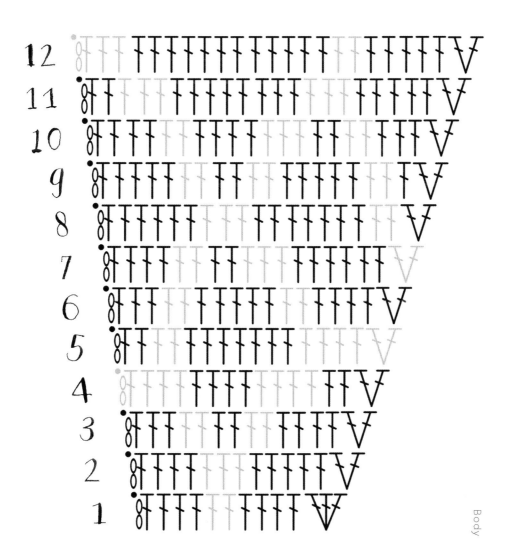

Body

Rnd 12: With yellow: ch2, *with yellow: dc3, with brown: dc12, with yellow: dc2, with brown: dc5, ch14, dc1 in 3rd ch from hook, dc1 in each of the remaining 11 chains, 2dc in next stitch of rnd 11*, repeat one more time, sl st in first dc.

Cut a long tail to close the body later.

PUTTING IT ALL TOGETHER

- Fold the body in line with the increases to make the belly straight and sew closed with the remaining yarn. Tie a knot in the corners to form the feet.
- Sew an arm to each side of the body in between rnds 1 and 2.
- Finally, sew rnd 12 of the head to rnd 1 of the body.

KOKESHI

DIFFICULTY LEVEL: 3 of 5

SIZE: 12 in (30 cm) tall

MATERIALS

Yarn: DK #3 light weight yarn; shown in Scheepjes Stone Washed

For girl:
- Bright pink (Red Jasper): 131 yd (120 m)
- Light pink (Pink Quartz-ite 821): 87.5 yd (80 m)
- Black (Black Onyx 803): 54.5 yd (50 m)
- Light blue (Amazonite 813): 33 yd (30 m)

For boy:
- Dark blue (Blue Apatite 805): 131 yd (120 m)
- Light pink (Pink Quartz-ite 821): 87.5 yd (80 m)
- Black (Black Onyx 803): 54.5 yd (50 m)
- Gold (Yellow Jasper 809): 33 yd (30 m)

Crochet hook: US size D-3 (3 mm)

Other:
- Small piece of black embroidery yarn or thin cotton yarn to embroider eyes
- Fiberfill stuffing
- Needle and scissors

HEAD (GIRL)

Rnd 1: With black: start with a magic ring, 6sc in the ring. (6)
Rnd 2: 2sc in each stitch around. (12)
Rnd 3: *Sc1, 2sc in next*, repeat around. (18)
Rnd 4: *Sc2, 2sc in next*, repeat around. (24)
Rnds 5–7: Sc1 in each stitch around. (24)
Rnd 8: *Sc2, sc2tog*, repeat around. (18)
Rnd 9: *Sc2, 2sc in next*, repeat around. (24)
Rnd 10: *Sc3, 2sc in next*, repeat around. (30)
Rnd 11: *Sc4, 2sc in next*, repeat around. (36)
Rnd 12: *Sc5, 2sc in next*, repeat around. (42)
Rnd 13: *Sc6, 2sc in next*, repeat around. (48)
Rnds 14–18: Sc1 in each stitch around. (48)
Rnd 19: With light pink: sc11, with black: sc37. (48)
Rnd 20: With light pink: sc12, with black: sc36. (48)
Rnd 21: With light pink: sc13, with black: sc35. (48)
Rnd 22: With light pink: sc14, with black: sc34. (48)
Rnd 23: With light pink: sc15, with black: sc33. (48)
Rnd 24: With light pink: sc16, with black: sc32. (48)
Rnd 25: With light pink: sc17, with black: sc31. (48)

Cut the black yarn.

Rnd 26: With light pink: *sc6, sc2tog*, repeat around. (42)
Rnd 27: *Sc5, sc2tog*, repeat around. (36)
Rnd 28: *Sc4, sc2tog*, repeat around. (30)
Rnd 29: *Sc3, sc2tog*, repeat around. (24)
Rnd 30: *Sc2, sc2tog*, repeat around. (18)
Rnd 31: *Sc1, sc2tog*, repeat around. (12)

Stuff the head.

Rnd 32: *Sc2tog*, repeat around. (6)

Cut yarn, weave through the 6 remaining stitches, pull tight, and weave in ends.

HEAD (BOY)

Rnd 1: With black: start with a magic ring, 6sc in the ring. (6)
Rnd 2: 2sc in each stitch around. (12)
Rnd 3: *Sc1, 2sc in next*, repeat around. (18)
Rnd 4: *Sc2, 2sc in next*, repeat around. (24)
Rnd 5: *Sc3, 2sc in next*, repeat around. (30)
Rnd 6: *Sc4, 2sc in next*, repeat around. (36)
Rnd 7: *Sc5, 2sc in next*, repeat around. (42)
Rnd 8: *Sc6, 2sc in next*, repeat around. (48)
Rnds 9–10: Sc1 in each stitch around. (48)
Rnd 11: With light pink: sc11, with black: sc37. (48)
Rnd 12: With light pink: sc12, with black: sc36. (48)
Rnd 13: With light pink: sc13, with black: sc35. (48)
Rnd 14: With light pink: sc14, with black: sc34. (48)
Rnd 15: With light pink: sc15, with black: sc33. (48)
Rnd 16: With light pink: sc16, with black: sc32. (48)
Rnd 17: With light pink: sc17, with black: sc31. (48)

Cut the black yarn.

Rnd 18: With light pink. *sc6, sc2tog*, repeat around. (42)
Rnd 19: *Sc5, sc2tog*, repeat around. (36)
Rnd 20: *Sc4, sc2tog*, repeat around. (30)
Rnd 21: *Sc3, sc2tog*, repeat around. (24)
Rnd 22: *Sc2, sc2tog*, repeat around. (18)
Rnd 23: *Sc1, sc2tog*, repeat around. (12)

Stuff the head.

Rnd 24: *Sc2tog*, repeat around. (6)

Cut yarn, weave through the 6 remaining stitches, pull tight, and weave in ends.

BODY

Rnd 1: With bright pink or dark blue: ch18, 1dc in 3rd ch from hook, dc14, 3dc in last, continue along other side of chain, dc15, 3dc in last, sl st in first dc. (36)
Rnd 2: Ch2 (doesn't count as first stitch now and throughout), *dc17, 2dc in next*, repeat one more time, sl st in first dc. (38)
Rnd 3: Ch2, *dc18, 2dc in next*, repeat one more time, sl st in first dc. (40)
Rnd 4: Ch2, *dc19, 2dc in next*, repeat one more time, sl st in first dc. (42)
Rnd 5: Ch2, *dc20, 2dc in next*, repeat one more time, sl st in first dc. (44)
Rnd 6: Ch2, *dc21, 2dc in next*, repeat one more time, sl st in first dc. (46)
Rnd 7: Ch2, *dc22, 2dc in next*, repeat one more time, sl st in first dc. (48)
Rnd 8: Change to light blue or gold. Ch2, *dc23, 2dc in next*, repeat one more time, sl st in first dc. (50)

Cut the light blue or gold yarn.

Rnd 9: Continue with bright pink or dark blue: ch2, *dc24, 2dc in next*, repeat one more time, sl st in first dc. (52)
Rnd 10: Ch2, *dc25, 2dc in next*, repeat one more time, sl st in first dc. (54)

Rnd 11: Ch2, *dc26, 2dc in next*, repeat one more time, sl st in first dc. (56)

Rnd 12: Ch2, *dc27, 2dc in next*, repeat one more time, sl st in first dc. (58)

Rnd 13: Ch2, *dc28, 2dc in next*, repeat one more time, sl st in first dc. (60)

Rnd 14: Ch2, *dc29, 2dc in next*, repeat one more time, sl st in first dc. (62)

Rnd 15: Ch2, *dc30, 2dc in next*, repeat one more time, sl st in first dc. (64)

Rnd 16: Ch2, *dc31, 2dc in next*, repeat one more time, sl st in first dc. (66)

Rnd 17: Ch2, *dc32, 2dc in next*, repeat one more time, sl st in first dc. (68)

Rnd 18: Ch2, *dc33, 2dc in next*, repeat one more time, sl st in first dc. (70)

Cut a long tail to close the body later. Fold the body in line with the increases to make the belly straight.

ARMS (MAKE 2)

Rnd 1: With light pink: start with a magic loop, 6sc in the loop. (6)

Rnd 2: 2sc in each stitch around. (12)

Rnd 3: *Sc1, 2sc in next*, repeat around. (18)

Rnds 4–10: Sc1 in each stitch around. (18)

Cut a long tail; you'll use it after rnd 12.

Rnd 11: With bright pink or dark blue, sl st 1, ch2 (doesn't count as first stitch now and throughout), dc in each stitch around, sl st in first dc. (18)

Rnd 12: Ch2, dc2tog, dc in each stitch around, sl st in first dc. (17)

At this point, stuff the hand. Take the remaining light pink yarn and sew across the arm between rnds 10 and 11.

Rnd 13: In back loops only, ch2, dc in each stitch around, sl st in first dc. (17)

Rnd 14: Ch2, dc2tog, dc in each stitch around, sl st in first dc. (16)

Rnd 15: Ch2, dc in each stitch around, sl st in first dc. (16)

Rnd 16: Ch2, dc2tog, dc in each stitch around, sl st in first dc. (15)

Rnd 17: Ch2, dc in each stitch around, sl st in first dc. (15)

Rnd 18: Ch2, dc2tog, dc in each stitch around, sl st in first dc. (14)

Rnd 19: Ch2, dc in each stitch around, sl st in first dc. (14)

Cut a long tail to attach arms to body later. Continue with instructions below for wide sleeves.

SLEEVES

Rnd 1: With bright pink or dark blue, with arm pointing toward you and hand pointing away, attach yarn in last unworked front loop of rnd 12 and continue working the rest of the unworked loops. Ch2, dc16, 3dc in last stitch, sl st in first dc. (19)

Rnd 2: Ch2, dc16, 2dc in each of the next 3 stitches, sl st in first dc. (22)

Rnd 3: With light blue or gold, ch2, dc16, 2dc in each of the next 6 stitches, sl st in first dc. (28)

Cut yarn and weave in ends.

FEET (MAKE 2)

Rnd 1: With light blue or gold: start with a magic loop, ch2 (doesn't count as first dc), dc12 in the loop, sl st in first dc. (12)

Rnd 2: Ch2, *dc1, 2dc in next*, repeat around, sl st in first dc. (18)

Rnd 3: Ch2, dc in each stitch around, sl st in first dc. (18)

Cut yarn and weave in ends.

/ / / / / / / | / | | / / / / | / / | | / / | | | / / | | |

PUTTING IT ALL TOGETHER

- Embroider eyes on each side of the face between rnds 21 and 23 for the girl and between rnds 13 and 15 for the boy.
- Sew the head (rnd 25 for the girl and rnd 19 for the boy) to rnd 1 of the body.
- Take the light blue or gold yarn and ch45, starting from the center of the light blue or gold band around the body, wrap around the neck and bring back to the starting point, and sew in place.
- Take the body and place both legs between the bottom two layers. With the remaining yarn from the body, sew across the seam with the legs in between. This way you close the bottom and assemble pieces at the same time.
- Sew an arm to each side of the body between rnds 1 and 3.
- Only for the girl: Take a small piece of light blue yarn, wrap 3 times around the bun, and sew in place.

BABY KOKESHI

DIFFICULTY LEVEL: 3 of 5

SIZE: 7 in (18 cm) tall

MATERIALS

Yarn: DK #3 light weight yarn; shown in Scheepjes Stone Washed

For girl:
- Bright pink (Red Jasper): 87.5 yd (80 m)
- Light pink (Pink Quartz-ite 821): 54.5 yd (50 m)
- Pink (Rose Quartz 820): 33 yd (30 m)
- Black (Black Onyx 803): 33 yd (30 m)

For boy:
- Dark blue (Blue Apatite 805): 97.5 yd (80 m)
- Light pink (Pink Quartz-ite 821): 54.5 yd (50 m)
- Black (Black Onyx 803): 33 yd (30 m)
- Light blue (Amazonite 813): 33 yd (30 m)

Crochet hook: US size D-3 (3 mm)

Other:
- Small piece of black embroidery yarn or thin cotton yarn to embroider eyes
- Fiberfill stuffing
- Needle and scissors

HEAD (GIRL)

Rnd 1: With black: start with a magic ring, 6sc in the ring. (6)

Rnd 2: 2sc in each stitch around. (12)

Rnd 3: *Sc1, 2sc in next*, repeat around. (18)

Rnds 4–5: Sc1 in each stitch around. (18)

Rnd 6: *Sc1, sc2tog*, repeat around. (12)

Rnd 7: *Sc1, 2sc in next*, repeat around. (18)

Rnd 8: *Sc2, 2sc in next*, repeat around. (24)

Rnd 9: *Sc3, 2sc in next*, repeat around. (30)

Rnd 10: *Sc4, 2sc in next*, repeat around. (36)

Rnds 11–12: Sc1 in each stitch around. (36)

Rnd 13: With light pink: sc7, with black: sc29. (36)

Rnd 14: With light pink: sc8, with black: sc28. (36)

Rnd 15: With light pink: sc9, with black: sc27. (36)

Rnd 16: With light pink: sc10, with black: sc26. (36)

Rnd 17: With light pink: sc11, with black: sc25. (36)

Rnd 18: With light pink: *sc4, sc2tog*, repeat from * to * one more time, with black: *sc4, sc2tog*, repeat to end (30)

Cut the black yarn.

Rnd 19: With light pink: *sc3, sc2tog*, repeat around. (24)

Rnd 20: *Sc2, sc2tog*, repeat around. (18)

Rnd 21: *Sc1, sc2tog*, repeat around. (12)

Stuff the head.

Rnd 22: *Sc2tog*, repeat around. (6)

Cut yarn, weave through the 6 remaining stitches, pull tight, and weave in ends.

HEAD (BOY)

Rnd 1: With black: start with a magic ring, 6sc in the ring. (6)
Rnd 2: 2sc in each stitch around. (12)
Rnd 3: *Sc1, 2sc in next*, repeat around. (18)
Rnd 4: *Sc2, 2sc in next*, repeat around. (24)
Rnd 5: *Sc3, 2sc in next*, repeat around. (30)
Rnd 6: *Sc4, 2sc in next*, repeat around. (36)
Rnds 7–8: Sc1 in each stitch around. (36)
Rnd 9: With light pink: sc7, with black: sc29. (36)
Rnd 10: With light pink: sc8, with black: sc28. (36)
Rnd 11: With light pink: sc9, with black: sc27. (36)
Rnd 12: With light pink: sc10, with black: sc26. (36)
Rnd 13: With light pink: sc11, with black: sc25. (36)
Rnd 14: With light pink: *sc4, sc2tog*, repeat from * to * one more time, with black: *sc4, sc2tog*, repeat to end. (30)

Cut the black yarn.

Rnd 15: With light pink: *sc3, sc2tog*, repeat around. (24)
Rnd 16: *Sc2, sc2tog*, repeat around. (18)
Rnd 17: *Sc1, sc2tog*, repeat around. (12)

Stuff the head.

Rnd 18: *Sc2tog*, repeat around. (6)

Cut yarn, weave through the 6 remaining stitches, pull tight, and weave in ends.

BODY

Rnd 1: With bright pink or dark blue: ch13, dc1 in 3rd ch from hook, dc9, 3dc in last, continue along the other side of the chains, dc10, 3dc in last, sl st in first dc. (26)

Rnd 2: Ch2 (doesn't count as first stitch now and throughout), *dc12, 2dc in next*, repeat one more time, sl st in first dc. (28)
Rnd 3: Ch2, *dc13, 2dc in next*, repeat one more time, sl st in first dc. (30)
Rnd 4: Ch2, *dc14, 2dc in next*, repeat one more time, sl st in first dc. (32)
Rnd 5: Ch2, *dc15, 2dc in next*, repeat one more time, sl st in first dc. (34)
Rnd 6: Continue with pink or light blue: ch2, *dc16, 2dc in next*, repeat one more time, sl st in first dc. (36)

Cut the pink or light blue yarn.

Rnd 7: Continue with bright pink or dark blue: ch2, *dc17, 2dc in next*, repeat one more time, sl st in first dc. (38)
Rnd 8: Ch2, *dc18, 2dc in next*, repeat one more time, sl st in first dc. (40)
Rnd 9: Ch2, *dc19, 2dc in next*, repeat one more time, sl st in first dc. (42)
Rnd 10: Ch2, *dc20, 2dc in next*, repeat one more time, sl st in first dc. (44)
Rnd 11: Ch2, *dc21, 2dc in next*, repeat one more time, sl st in first dc. (46)
Rnd 12: Ch2, *dc22, ch14, dc1 in 3rd ch from hook, dc1 in each of the remaining 11 chains, 2dc in next stitch of rnd 11*, repeat one more time, sl st in first dc.

Cut a long tail to close the body later.

ARMS (MAKE 2)

Rnd 1: With light pink: start with a magic loop, 6sc in the loop. (6)
Rnd 2: 2sc in each stitch around. (12)
Rnd 3: *Sc1, 2sc in next*, repeat around. (18)
Rnds 4–5: Sc1 in each stitch around. (18)
Rnd 6: *Sc1, sc2tog*, repeat around. (12)
Rnd 7: Sc1 in each stitch around. (12)

Cut a long tail; you'll use it after rnd 9.

Rnd 8: With bright pink or dark blue, sl st 1, ch2 (doesn't count as first stitch now and through-out), dc in each stitch around, sl st in first dc. (12)

Rnd 9: Ch2, dc2tog, dc in each stitch around, sl st in first dc. (11)

At this point, stuff the hand. Take the remaining light pink yarn and sew across the arm between rnds 7 and 8.

Rnd 10: In back loops only, ch2, dc in each stitch around, sl st in first dc. (11)

Rnd 11: Ch2, dc2tog, dc in each stitch around, sl st in first dc. (10)

Rnd 12: Ch2, dc in each stitch around, sl st in first dc. (10)

Cut a long tail to attach arms to body later. Continue with instructions below for wide sleeves.

SLEEVES

Rnd 1: With bright pink or dark blue, with arm pointing toward you and hand pointing away, attach yarn in last unworked front loop of rnd 9 and continue working the rest of the un-worked loops. Ch2, dc10, 3dc in last stitch, sl st in first dc. (13)

Rnd 2: Ch2, dc10, 2dc in each of the next 3 stitch-es, sl st in first dc. (16)

Rnd 3: With pink or light blue, ch2, dc10, 2dc in each of the next 6 stitches, sl st in first dc. (22)

Cut yarn and weave in ends.

PUTTING IT ALL TOGETHER

- Embroider eyes on each side of the face between rnds 14 and 16 for the girl and between rnds 10 and 12 for the boy.
- Sew the head (rnd 20 for the girl and rnd 16 for the boy) to rnd 1 of the body.
- Take the pink or light blue yarn and ch35 starting from the center of the pink or light blue band around the body, wrap around the neck and bring back to the starting point, and sew in place.
- Fold the body in line with the increas-es to make the belly straight and sew closed with the remaining yarn. Tie a knot in the corners to form the feet.
- Sew an arm to each side of the body in between rnds 1 and 2.
- Only for the girl: Take a red pencil or a little rouge and add little cheeks below the outer corner of the eye.
- Only for the girl: Take a small piece of pink yarn, wrap 3 times around the bun, and sew in place.

FLAMINGO

DIFFICULTY LEVEL: 2 of 5

SIZE: 17.5 in (45 cm) tall

MATERIALS

Yarn: DK #3 light weight yarn; shown in Scheepjes Stone Washed
- Pink (Rose Quartz 820): 142 yd (130 m)
- Red (Carnelian 823): 87.5 yd (80 m)
- White (Moon Stone 801): 54.5 yd (50 m)

Crochet hook: US size D-3 (3 mm)

Other:
- Black and gold safety eyes, 15 mm
- Fiberfill stuffing
- Needle and scissors

HEAD AND BODY

Rnd 1: With white: start with a magic loop, 6sc in the loop. (6)
Rnd 2: Sc1 in each stitch around. (6)
Rnd 3: 2sc in each of next 2 stitches, 4sc. (8)
Rnd 4: Sc1 in each stitch around. (8)
Rnd 5: *Sc1, 2sc in next stitch*, repeat from * to * one more time, sc4. (10)
Rnd 6: Sc1 in each stitch around. (10)
Rnd 7: *Sc1, 2sc in next stitch*, repeat from * to * one more time, sc6. (12)
Rnd 8: Sc1 in each stitch around. (12)
Rnd 9: *Sc1, 2sc in next stitch*, repeat from * to * one more time, sc8. (14)
Rnd 10: Sc1 in each stitch around. (14)
Rnd 11: *Sc1, 2sc in next stitch*, repeat from * to * one more time, sc10. (16)
Rnd 12: Sc1 in each stitch around. (16)
Rnd 13: *Sc1, 2sc in next stitch*, repeat from * to * one more time, sc12. (18)
Rnd 14: Sc1 in each stitch around. (18)
Rnd 15: *Sc2, 2sc in next stitch*, repeat from * to * around. (24)

Cut the white yarn.

Rnd 16: Continue with pink: *sc3, 2sc in next stitch*, repeat from * to * around. (30)
Rnd 17: *Sc4, 2sc in next stitch*, repeat from * to * around. (36)

Rnds 18–29: Sc1 in each stitch around. (36)

Attach the safety eyes between rnds 17 and 18 on each side of the beak, 11 stitches apart. Stuff the beak; I did this by just adding little pieces each time and stuffing them with the back of my hook. Pay close attention to the shape of the beak, making it slightly curved and even, without bumps.

Rnd 30: *Sc4, sc2tog*, repeat from * to * around. (30)
Rnd 31: *Sc3, sc2tog*, repeat from * to * around. (24)
Rnd 32: *Sc2, sc2tog*, repeat from * to * around. (18)

Stuff the head firmly.

Rnd 33: Sl st 1, ch2 (doesn't count as first stitch now and throughout so the first dc is made in the same stitch as the previous ch2), dc1 in each stitch around, sl st in first dc. (18)
Rnd 34: Ch2, dc1 in each stitch around, sl st in first dc. (18)

Take a small piece of pink yarn, fold rnds 33 and 34 flat, make sure the eyes are even on top, and then sew the line between rnds 32 and 33 to divide the head and neck section and keep the stuffing in the head.

Rnds 35–44: Ch2, dc1 in each stitch around, sl st in first dc. (18)
Rnd 45: Ch2, *dc5, 2dc in next stitch*, repeat from * to * around, sl st in first dc. (21)
Rnd 46: Ch2, *dc6, 2dc in next stitch*, repeat from * to * around, sl st in first dc. (24)
Rnd 47: Ch2, *dc7, 2dc in next stitch*, repeat from * to * around, sl st in first dc. (27)
Rnd 48: Ch2, *dc8, 2dc in next stitch*, repeat from * to * around, sl st in first dc. (30)
Rnd 49: Ch2, *dc9, 2dc in next stitch*, repeat from * to * around, sl st in first dc. (33)

Rnd 50: Ch2, *dc10, 2dc in next stitch*, repeat from * to * around, sl st in first dc. (36)
Rnd 51: Ch2, *dc11, 2dc in next stitch*, repeat from * to * around, sl st in first dc. (39)
Rnd 52: Ch2, *dc12, 2dc in next stitch*, repeat from * to * around, sl st in first dc. (42)
Rnd 53: Ch2, *dc6, 2dc in next stitch*, repeat from * to * around, sl st in first dc. (48)
Rnd 54: Ch2, *dc7, 2dc in next stitch*, repeat from * to * around, sl st in first dc. (54)
Rnd 55: Ch2, *dc8, 2dc in next stitch*, repeat from * to * around, sl st in first dc. (60)
Rnd 56: Ch2, *dc9, 2dc in next stitch*, repeat from * to * around, sl st in first dc. (66)
Rnds 57–61: Ch2, dc1 in each stitch around, sl st in first dc. (66)
Rnd 62: Ch2, *dc9, dc2tog*, repeat from * to * around, sl st in first dc. (60)
Rnd 63: Ch2, *dc8, dc2tog*, repeat from * to * around, sl st in first dc. (54)
Rnd 64: Ch2, *dc7, dc2tog*, repeat from * to * around, sl st in first dc. (48)
Rnd 65: Ch2, *dc6, dc2tog*, repeat from * to * around, sl st in first dc. (42)
Rnd 66: Ch2, *dc5, dc2tog*, repeat from * to * around, sl st in first dc. (36)
Rnd 67: Ch2, *dc4, dc2tog*, repeat from * to * around, sl st in first dc. (30)
Rnd 68: Ch2, *dc3, dc2tog*, repeat from * to * around, sl st in first dc. (24)
Rnd 69: Ch2, *dc2, dc2tog*, repeat from * to * around, sl st in first dc. (18)
Rnd 70: Ch2, *dc4, dc2tog*, repeat from * to * around, sl st in first dc. (15)
Rnd 71: Ch2, *dc3, dc2tog*, repeat from * to * around, sl st in first dc. (12)
Rnd 72: Ch2, *dc1, dc2tog*, repeat from * to * around, sl st in first dc. (8)
Rnd 73: Ch2, *dc2tog*, repeat from * to * around, sl st in first dc. (4)

Cut yarn and weave in ends.

WINGS (MAKE 2)

Rnd 1: With red: start with a magic loop, ch2 (doesn't count as first stitch now and through-out), 6dc in the loop, sl st in first dc. (6)

Rnd 2: Ch2, 2dc in each stitch around, sl st in first dc. (12)

Rnd 3: Ch2, *dc1, 2dc in next*, repeat around, sl st in first dc. (18)

Rnd 4: Ch2, *dc2, 2dc in next*, repeat around, sl st in first dc. (24)

Rnd 5: Ch2, dc1 in each stitch around, sl st in first dc. (24)

Rnd 6: Ch2, *dc2, dc2tog*, repeat 2 more times (3 decreases in total), dc12, sl st in first dc. (21)

Rnd 7: Ch2, dc1 in each stitch around, sl st in first dc. (21)

Rnd 8: Ch2, *dc1, dc2tog*, repeat 2 more times (3 decreases in total), dc12, sl st in first dc. (18)

Rnd 9: Ch2, dc1 in each stitch around, sl st in first dc. (18)

Rnd 10: Ch2, dc2tog 3 times (3 decreases in to-tal), dc12, sl st in first dc. (15)

Rnd 11: Ch2, dc1 in each stitch around, sl st in first dc. (15)

Cut a long tail to attach wings in the end.

LEGS (MAKE 2)

Rnd 1: With red: start with a magic loop, ch2 (doesn't count as first stitch now and through-out), 8dc in the loop, sl st in first dc. (8)

Rnds 2–5: Ch2, dc1 in each stitch around, sl st in first dc. (8)

Rnd 6: Ch2, 2dc in each stitch around, sl st in first dc. (16)

Rnd 7: Ch2, *dc2tog*, repeat from * to * around, sl st in first dc. (8)

Rnds 8–9: Ch2, dc1 in each stitch around, sl st in first dc. (8)

From now on, you'll continue working in rnds without closing them.

Rnd 10: 2sc in each stitch around. (16)

Rnd 11: *Sc1, 2sc in next*, repeat around. (24)

Rnds 12–16: Sc1 in each stitch around. (24)

Rnd 17: *Sc1, (in next sc: 1hdc, 1dc, 1tr, 1dc, 1hdc), sc1, sl st 1*, repeat from * to * around.

You'll have 3 toes (6 repeats). Cut a long tail and sew the seam of the toes closed.

PUTTING IT ALL TOGETHER

- Sew the wings to each side of the body between rnds 50 and 53.
- Sew rnd 1 of each leg to each side of the body in between rnds 65 and 66.

BABY FLAMINGO

DIFFICULTY LEVEL: 2 of 5

SIZE: 8 in (21 cm) tall

MATERIALS

Yarn: DK #3 light weight yarn;
shown in Scheepjes Stone
Washed
- Red (Carnelian 823):
  65.5 yd (60 m)
- White (Moon Stone 801):
  54.5 yd (50 m)
- Pink (Rose Quartz 820):
  44 yd (40 m)

DK #3 light weight furry yarn;
shown in Scheepjes Softy (if
you don't have furry yarn,
continue with pink)
- Pink (Rose 496): 76.5 yd
  (70 m)

Crochet hook: US size D-3
(3 mm)

Other:
- Black and gold safety
  eyes, 12 mm
- Fiberfill stuffing
- Needle and scissors

HEAD AND BODY

Rnd 1: With white: start with a magic loop, 6sc in
the loop. (6)

Rnd 2: Sc1 in each stitch around. (6)

Rnd 3: 2sc in each of next 2 stitches, sc4. (8)

Rnd 4: Sc1 in each stitch around. (8)

Rnd 5: 2sc in each of next 2 stitches, sc6. (10)

Rnd 6: Sc1 in each stitch around. (10)

Rnd 7: 2sc in each of next 2 stitches, sc8. (12)

Rnd 8: *Sc1, 2sc in next stitch*, repeat from * to *
around. (18)

Cut the white yarn and continue with pink.

Rnd 9: *Sc2, 2sc in next stitch*, repeat from * to *
around. (24)

Rnds 10–17: Sc1 in each stitch around. (24)

Attach the safety eyes between rnds 10 and 11
on each side of the beak, 6 stitches apart. Stuff
the beak; I did this by just adding little pieces
at a time and stuffing them with the back of my
hook. Pay close attention to the shape of the
beak, making it slightly curved and even, without
bumps.

Rnd 18: *Sc2, sc2tog*, repeat from * to * around.
(18)

Rnd 19: *Sc1, sc2tog*, repeat from * to * around.
(12)

Stuff the head firmly.

Rnd 20: Sl st 1, ch2 (doesn't count as first stitch now and throughout so the first dc is made in the same stitch as the previous ch2), dc1 in each stitch around, sl st in first dc. (12)

Rnd 21: Ch2, dc1 in each stitch around, sl st in first dc. (12)

Take a small piece of pink yarn, fold rnds 20 and 21 flat, make sure the eyes are evenly on top, and then sew a line between rnds 19 and 20 to divide the head and neck section and keep the stuffing in the head.

Rnds 22–30: Ch2, dc1 in each stitch around, sl st in first dc. (12)

If you want to make the body with furry yarn, this is the point to change yarns. Otherwise, continue with pink.

Rnd 31: Ch2, *dc3, 2dc in next stitch*, repeat from * to * around, sl st in first dc. (15)

Rnd 32: Ch2, *dc4, 2dc in next stitch*, repeat from * to * around, sl st in first dc. (18)

Rnd 33: Ch2, *dc5, 2dc in next stitch*, repeat from * to * around, sl st in first dc. (21)

Rnd 34: Ch2, *dc6, 2dc in next stitch*, repeat from * to * around, sl st in first dc. (24)

Rnd 35: Ch2, *dc7, 2dc in next stitch*, repeat from * to * around, sl st in first dc. (27)

Rnd 36: Ch2, *dc8, 2dc in next stitch*, repeat from * to * around, sl st in first dc. (30)

Rnd 37: Ch2, *dc9, 2dc in next stitch*, repeat from * to * around, sl st in first dc. (33)

Rnd 38: Ch2, *dc10, 2dc in next stitch*, repeat from * to * around, sl st in first dc. (36)

Rnds 39–40: Ch2, dc1 in each stitch around, sl st in first dc. (36)

Rnd 41: Ch2, *dc4, dc2tog*, repeat from * to * around, sl st in first dc. (30)

Rnd 42: Ch2, *dc3, dc2tog*, repeat from * to * around, sl st in first dc. (24)

Rnd 43: Ch2, *dc2, dc2tog*, repeat from * to * around, sl st in first dc. (18)

Rnd 44: Ch2, *dc4, dc2tog*, repeat from * to * around, sl st in first dc. (15)

Rnd 45: Ch2, *dc3, dc2tog*, repeat from * to * around, sl st in first dc. (12)

Rnd 46: Ch2, *dc1, dc2tog*, repeat from * to * around, sl st in first dc. (8)

Rnd 47: Ch2, *dc2tog*, repeat from * to * around, sl st in first dc. (4)

Cut yarn and weave in ends.

WINGS (MAKE 2)

Rnd 1: With red, start with a magic ring, ch2, 6dc in the ring, sl st in first dc. (6)

Rnd 2: Ch2, 2dc in each stitch around, sl st in first dc. (12)

Rnd 3: Ch2, *dc1, 2dc in next*, repeat around, sl st in first dc. (18)

Rnd 4: Ch2, dc in each stitch around, sl st in first dc. (18)

Rnd 5: Ch2, *dc1, dc2tog*, repeat 2 more times (3 decreases in total), dc9, sl st in first dc. (15)

Rnd 6: Ch2, dc in each stitch around, sl st in first dc. (15)

Rnd 7: Ch2, dc2tog three times (3 decreases in total), dc9, sl st in first dc. (12)

Rnd 8: Ch2, dc in each stitch around, sl st in first dc. (12)

Cut a long tail to attach wings in the end.

LEGS (MAKE 2)

Rnd 1: With red, start with a magic loop, ch2 (doesn't count as first stitch now and throughout), 6dc in the loop, sl st in first dc. (6)

Rnd 2: Ch2, dc1 in each stitch around, sl st in first dc. (6)

Rnd 3: Ch2, 2dc in each stitch around, sl st in first dc. (12)

Rnd 4: Ch2, *dc2tog*, repeat from * to * around, sl st in first dc. (6)

Rnds 5–6: Ch2, dc1 in each stitch around, sl st in first dc. (6)

From now on you'll continue working in rnds without closing them.

Rnd 7: 2sc in each stitch around. (12)

Rnd 8: *Sc1, 2sc in next*, repeat around. (18)

Rnd 9: Sc in each stitch around. (18)

Rnd 10: *Sc1, (in next: hdc1, dc1, tr1, dc1, hdc1), sl st 1*, repeat around.

You'll end up with 3 toes (6 repeats). Cut a long tail to close the seam of the feet at the end.

PUTTING IT ALL TOGETHER

- Sew the wings to each side of the body between rnds 32 and 33.
- Sew rnd 1 of each leg to each side of the body in rnd 45.

ACKNOWLEDGMENTS

This is already the last page of the book! It is a very proud moment in this challenging, intensive but, above all, beautiful period.

This book demonstrates a period of growth that you can literally see in the pictures of my growing children: Mijntje, who has experienced this whole adventure with me and grew up from a young child between the ragdolls, to a beautiful young lady who now has her brother on her lap! Julia, who appeared in the very first book as a toddler and now, like a real model, loves the camera. Olivier, who just came to watch, but is a big fan of the ragdolls and gives them a kiss every day! And all that with, in the background, my husband, Josse—my rock, through thick and thin. Without you, I would never have come this far!

My dear parents, parents-in-law, brother and sister-in-law, thank you for all the support, love, and wise advice! My brothers-in-law, sisters-in-law, aunts, uncles, and all family, thank you for your support!

In addition, there are many people who have helped enormously in the production of this book!

Ans Baart, my original thank-you texts are starting to run out, but that's also because I'm grateful to you for so much! For your support, your friendship, your endless commitment to my designs and patterns, thank you!

Dennis de Gussem, dear perfectionist, thank you for testing and crocheting for this book! I am very grateful for your help and commitment!

Also a huge thank-you to all the testers who tested these patterns with so much love and dedication! Bianca van der Maarel, Chantal Put-Schoutene, Colette Hendriks, Corina van Krieken, Diane van Lier-Noordenbos, Emanuelle Overeem, Eveline Hartog, Eveline Koeleman, Joke Stuurman, Karin Frenzen, Lisa van de Graaf-Slootman, Monique Schut, Sofie de Zutter, Tine Oetzman. And my English-speaking testers: Morea Petersen, Annie Shelton, Lindsey Mae Strippelhoff, Debbie Allen Richardson, Leslie Mansfield, Emily Truman, Yee Wong, Mandy Jo and Grace Dunlap

Esther Befort, this is already our eighth book together! I still marvel that you can capture my thoughts exactly as I envisioned them. Thank you again for the beautiful photos, your support, and your creativity!

Sigrid Bliekendaal, you helped take my books to a new level. I have learned a lot from you, and I am very grateful for that!

Kosmos Publishers, and in particular, Marieke Woortman and Sabine Meekel, thank you for making this book possible. I hope we can publish many more books together!

I also want to thank Stackpole Books and in particular Candi Derr for giving me the opportunity to publish this translation. I am very grateful for this publication and all of your great work and dedication.

Julia Foldenyi and Irina Fomichev, thank you both so much for all of your help and guidance in the process of translations.

Jeanet Jaffari-Schroevers, thank you for the beautiful yarns, your support, and your contribution!

Bert Noorderijk, thank you for helping me realize my dreams!

Kristel Neuckens, thank you for your support and trust!

Lineke Vrieling-van Dijk, thank you for making the Scheepjes yarns available for years and for your support!

Allan Marshal, thank you so much for the beautiful crochet hooks you've made for me!

Phaedra Tanghe, thank you for the beautiful handmade stitch markers!

Thank you, Debby Groeneveld, for your help and support on the Facebook groups, and also thank you to Peggy Jansen-Peters for your support and contribution!

In addition, there are many companies and their employees who have contributed to the materials for this book! Huge thanks for that!